The New Geography of Capital

The New Geography of Capitalism

Firms, Finance, and Society

Adam D. Dixon

OXFORD
UNIVERSITY PRESS

OXFORD
UNIVERSITY PRESS

Great Clarendon Street, Oxford, OX2 6DP,
United Kingdom

Oxford University Press is a department of the University of Oxford.
It furthers the University's objective of excellence in research, scholarship,
and education by publishing worldwide. Oxford is a registered trade mark of
Oxford University Press in the UK and in certain other countries

Published in the United States of America by Oxford University Press
198 Madison Avenue, New York, NY 10016, United States of America

British Library Cataloguing in Publication Data
Data available

Library of Congress Control Number: 2013957855

ISBN 978–0–19–966824–3

For Fay and Olga

Preface

The causes and consequences of the global financial crisis that began in the summer of 2007 have been told and retold by various commentators and through various media. For many in the social sciences not accustomed to taking global finance seriously or at least knowing what to make of it, the crisis has been a wake-up call. It reaffirmed a simple fact: finance pervades almost all aspects of contemporary economic activity and social life, from the way firms are managed, to the built environment of urban centers, and the prospects for one's quality of life in retirement. The intensity through which finance pervades contemporary economic life, a process which some refer to as financialization, suggests we have moved well beyond classic debates on the role of finance in economic growth and development. In certain parts of the world it may still be possible to interrogate whether finance leads development or simply follows in the wake of enterprising firms. But even those places are likely to be subsumed into wider global financial networks and processes, directly or indirectly, wherein the prospects of entire economies and regions are subject to the pricing power of the market.

As the prospects of individuals and entire countries have become intertwined with the performance of global financial markets, the crisis served to reinforce the enduring anxiety, both in the social sciences and the public sphere, over the authenticity and continued survival of social solidarity at various spatial scales, from the community to the nation-state. At the center of this anxiety, notwithstanding the increasing integration and political influence of financial markets and actors, is a rapidly changing geography of capitalism: one where cities and regions have re-emerged as the critical loci of the economic order in place of the nation-state; where the identity and loyalties of firms often transcend national borders; and where a middle class, whose prospects are less tied up with the success of the national economy than with some place afar, may find it increasingly difficult to align its interests with the less fortunate and within its own ranks.

To be sure, the organizing logic of the nation-state still claims legitimacy and relevance, as a crucial site of governance and regulation, and an incubator of cultural and linguistic tradition. Nonetheless, such legitimacy is juxtaposed with a strong unease over whether the nation-state has the capacity to deliver—consider the Eurozone sovereign debt crisis. Indeed, the changing geography of capitalism underpinned by an expanding global division of labor and the integration of financial markets has undercut the bordering logics necessary for the maintenance of national systems of production, national varieties of capitalism, and national systems of social protection. Put simply, the globalization of financial markets coupled with the globalization of supply chains through outsourcing and offshoring act in concert to liberate firms, the key loci of national production systems, from their history and geography. If the collective welfare of the nation-state relies on capturing the value of production, this new economic geography has made doing so increasingly complicated and difficult.

This changing geography of capitalism may not overcome completely the myriad ways nation-state political economies are organized and the institutions through which economic activity occurs. The economic landscape is still characterized by distinctive patterns of economic performance and well-being. Yet, the intensification of interdependence and the scope for formal and, more importantly, functional convergence in the action frameworks and incentive structures underpinning key institutions of capitalism, such as firms and financial systems, should not be understated. Hence, an intellectual challenge exists in formulating an analytical frame that adequately captures this changing geography of capitalism and the implications for economy and society, yet without advocating a one-world hyper-globalization vision of the global political–economic order. This book offers a contribution to addressing this challenge.

While sympathetic to the tradition of scholarship under the guise of "varieties of capitalism" or "social systems of production"—which is concerned with the comparative structure, function, and performance of national production systems and welfare-state regimes as comprehensive arrangements of interdependent institutions—this book offers a constructive challenge to the methodological nationalism of this tradition and the propensity at times to characterize change within and between economies and societies as a slow "path-dependent" process of incremental change. In this respect, while committed likewise to seeing economy and society as a whole, the approach here, rooted in economic geography, takes a realistic rather than idealistic view about the so-called "efficiency" of its parts. Accordingly, in this book is an argument about seeing economic and social processes at a variety of scales rather than privileging one scale as the unit of analysis or for that matter arguing that one scale is the proper place for governance and regulation.

In this manner, the aim of this book is to illuminate the challenges facing national systems of production and their associated national systems of social protection by analyzing finance in its various forms and functions, and its role in transforming the global economy. Theoretical support for this argument is drawn from two strands of research. First, I draw on scholarship in economic geography concerning the contemporary restructuring of the global economy around large city-regions, as fundamental drivers of economic growth and development. Second, theoretical support for explicating the significance of global financial integration is drawn from the burgeoning area of financial geography. This work has three interrelated foci: (1) understanding the geographical structure and scope of financial markets and the political–economic foundations of financial agents (e.g. institutional investors and investment banks); (2) understanding the capacity and scope of globally integrated financial markets and financial agents to price history and geography, and thus undercut the resilience of local institutional traditions (e.g. corporate governance), therefore driving or facilitating *formal* or at the least *functional* convergence in the process; (3) explicating the ways and means through which value is captured and concentrated across time and space by particular economic agents.

Ultimately, this book is about advancing an economic–geographical perspective for explaining the changing relationship between contemporary political economies, firms, and global financial markets. But this is not simply a book about economic geography. While this book makes a theoretical argument about the geography of capitalism in the twenty-first century, it does so utilizing and enrolling a range of literatures from across the social sciences. Besides, economic geography regularly engages outside of the sub-discipline for theoretical inspiration and support. As such, this book is interdisciplinary in its emphasis, its outlook, and its contribution to scholarship. On that point, an attempt has been made to present the material in an open and accessible manner such that it appeals to a wide audience, from undergraduates to career scholars.

What follows are six chapters that explore the changing geography of capitalism in relation to the firm, financial systems, and the welfare state. Although the empirical content of the book is primarily focused on advanced Western democracies, this does not limit the broader claims made about contemporary capitalism. The specific experiences of the advanced democracies discussed illustrate different issues and themes surrounding larger global developments. In that respect, the book is not an exhaustive treatise on capitalism and its changing geography, nor is it doctrinaire. Rather, it is intended as a contribution to a wider dialogue that includes multiple disciplines and multiple empirical contexts.

Given the central place of finance in the argument, Chapter 1 provides an analytical frame for explaining the geography of finance and global financial integration. The chapter unpacks the functions of finance, the form of financial systems, and the drivers of financial system convergence, as a means of evaluating similarities among geographically distinct financial systems and their integration with higher scales of aggregation. Our perspective rests on a view that institutional form does not necessarily determine function and that function does not necessarily determine institutional form—a view which is fleshed out further in Chapters 3 and 4. By breaking this causal assumption, this perspective of institutional form and function and institutional change avoids the potential pitfalls of methodological territorialism, which tends to hold history and geography static. Moreover, it injects a more spatially and temporally dynamic perspective into the analysis of the forces of economic integration and mimesis that are changing previously distinctive economic geographies across different scales.

Chapter 2 focuses on the economic geography of production. The title "One World of Production?" is purposively provocative. While partially hyperbolic, the point is to put in stark relief the challenge of conceptualizing national production systems in the face of global economic integration. It does so, in the first instance, by rehearsing scholarship in economic geography on the territorial development of capitalism in general and globalization in particular, restating the conceptualization of the landscape of global production as a global mosaic of regional systems of production and exchange. This allows for the continued appreciation of territorial specificity and institutional diversity, while eschewing a strong pretense toward methodological nationalism and a view of globalization as the spreading out of economic activity or the transformation of the economic order into a liquefied space of flows. The chapter integrates finance into this argument, considering how the pursuit of portfolio diversification and the demand for liquidity (i.e. the ease of exit) among international investors provide a mechanism for institutional change and convergence to occur. However, the chapter makes an argument that, while global finance is a powerful force driving convergence, modern global finance is in some ways tolerant of institutional variegation. It argues, on the one hand, that the principle of diversification demands differentiation, and on the other, that financial markets and actors frequently follow change emanating from other developments instead of acting as the instigators of such change.

Chapter 3 introduces a further element to our review and discussion of economic–geographical thought surrounding globalization by building on the concept of "variegated capitalism" through a perspective focused on the firm. This approach focuses on the temporality and spatiality of uneven capitalist development across political economies, viewing capitalism in the singular, and more importantly, as a dynamic polymorphic process whose development is uneven and "variegated." In this respect, capitalist variegation is understood as a more explicitly relational conception of variety, recognizing the strong and complex interdependencies present in global capitalist structuration and contingent institutional convergence among different so-called varieties of capitalism. As such, it provides a more nuanced appreciation of the place of firms in a global political–economic conjunction marked by the globalization of financial markets and the globalization of supply chains.

In Chapters 4, 5, and 6, the theoretical and conceptual arguments described in the first three chapters are extended and refined through more in-depth empirical analysis. Chapter 4 considers the treatment of institutions and institutional change in relation to finance, by contrasting the changing form and function since the beginning of the 1990s of the German financial system and banking sector with that of the United States. It is shown that the financial systems of the two countries are increasingly similar in form; and where they continue to diverge in form, common functions produce analogous outcomes. This complicates the modeling and empirical verification of capitalist variety at the national macro-institutional level. Consequently, there is a need for a re-evaluation of how and whether finance can continue to complement other institutional spheres within countries and in country-specific ways.

Chapter 5 considers the implications of the changing geography of capitalism for the nation-state's role in social protection, particularly in the area of public pensions. The chapter provides a brief history on the development of the welfare state, noting how it emerged under particular historical–geographical conditions, which no longer hold good. As national economies struggle to navigate and capture sufficient value from the new geography of production, retirement-income security has become increasingly dependent on the performance of financial markets. If welfare states have yet to converge on institutional form, this shift toward pre-funding pensions has resulted in increasing functional equivalence across different institutional environments. Hence, the restructuring of the welfare state toward a reliance on global financial markets, and the interdependence this brings, adds another element eroding the distinctive political–economic foundations of particular national economies. The chapter explores this shift in policy through the case of France.

Chapter 6 considers the changing role of the firm in systems of social protection. It does so through an examination of how and why firms have pulled back significantly in their provision of occupational defined benefit pensions, regardless of national traditions. Firms everywhere are largely unwilling to assume long-term liabilities associated with the provision of non-wage benefits. The decline of corporate-sponsored occupational defined benefit pensions is, in part, an outcome of the globalization of financial markets and the globalization of supply chains. Large firms in particular are hardly constrained by their history and geography. Notwithstanding this broader trend, the outcomes of this shift are still contingent on the local institutional environment. Such contingency is demonstrated by comparing the decline and transformation of occupational defined benefit pensions in the United Kingdom and the Netherlands.

The final chapter concludes our discussion, using the global financial crisis as its starting point.

Adam D. Dixon
Bristol, September 2013

Acknowledgements

The writing of this book occurred during a sabbatical year during which I was a recipient of a University Research Fellowship from the University of Bristol's Institute for Advanced Studies. My thanks go to the Institute and to the School of Geographical Sciences for facilitating my leave. My thanks also go to Johannes Glückler and the Institute of Geography at Heidelberg University for facilitating a three-month visit in the winter of 2013, and to Rob Bauer and the European Centre for Corporate Engagement at Maastricht University for facilitating a three-month visit in the spring of 2013. Both places provided a useful change of scenery and motivation to complete the project. I would like to give a special thanks to Ashby H. B. Monk and Ville-Pekka Sorsa, with whom I co-authored two papers, respectively, where some of the ideas herein were developed. I would like to thank Gordon L. Clark, Ewald Engelen, and an anonymous reviewer for providing constructive feedback on an earlier draft of the manuscript. Thanks also go to David Musson and Emma Booth at OUP for supporting the project along the way. None of the above should be held responsible for any errors or opinions expressed herein.

The arguments put forth in this book draw, in part, on ideas and material that were developed in a number of previously published journal articles. I wish to acknowledge the publishers of the original sources: John Wiley & Sons for "The geography of finance: form and functions," *Geography Compass* (2011) 5:851–862, DOI: 10.1111/j.1749-8198.2011.00458.x [ISSN: 1749-8198]; Maney Publishing for "Institutional change and the financialisation of pensions in Europe," *Competition &*

Change (2009) 13:347–367, DOI: 10.1179/102452909X1250691 5718111 [ISSN 1024-5294]; Oxford University Press for "Function before form: macro-institutional comparison and the geography of finance," *Journal of Economic Geography* (2012) 12:579–600, DOI:10.1093/jeg/lbr043 [ISSN 1468-2702], and "The power of finance: accounting harmonization's effect on pension provision," *Journal of Economic Geography* (2009) 9:619–639, DOI:10.1093/jeg/lbp018 [ISSN 1468-2702]; Sage for "Variegated capitalism and the geography of finance: towards a common agenda," *Progress in Human Geography* (2011) 35:193–210, DOI: 10.1177/0309132510372006 [ISSN 0309-1325]; and Taylor & Francis for "The rise of pension fund capitalism in Europe: an unseen revolution?" *New Political Economy* (2008) 13:249–270, DOI: 10.1080/13563460802302560 [ISSN 1356-3467].

Contents

List of Illustrations

Figures

Tables

1

The Geography of Finance

If one lesson can be drawn from the global financial crisis that began in the summer of 2007, it is that it reminded scholars of the extent and scope of financial interdependence across countries (Engelen and Faulconbridge 2009; Garretsen et al. 2009). Although the crisis was precipitated initially by the collapse of the subprime housing bubble in the United States, the subsequent financial and economic distress experienced in different countries, both developed and developing, unveiled the high degree to which finance has become entrenched in political–economic and sociocultural life (Leyshon and Thrift 2007; Martin 2011). Conceptualizing finance simply as the intermediation between suppliers and users of capital discounts the many ways finance, financial markets, and conventional financial practices have come to dominate corporate, governmental, and individual behavior, whether by choice, by force, or by necessity. It also discounts how finance is and has become a major source of scalar and spatial political–economic restructuring (Clark et al. 2009; Leyshon and Thrift 1997; Martin 1999).

In the face of geopolitical and economic integration it has become progressively more difficult to ascertain the form of national and/or regional financial systems. How do we know if a financial system is bank-based or market-based? Policy convergence in the form of common regulatory standards, for example, has eroded previous distinctions or opened financial systems to new practices and new actors. Or where the form of a financial system appears different, the functions and practices happening within that financial system may correspond with those of another financial system that is different in form; geographically specific political, social, and even cultural circumstances may reinforce formal institutional differences, but under the surface many practices and policies are not functionally different.

There is a further element of this analytical dilemma: scale. Where do the borders of one financial system stop and the borders of another begin? From about the beginning of the 1980s international capital flows, which include portfolio investment, have increased almost exponentially. As shown in Figure 1.1, while high-income countries dominate international capital flows, followed by the oil exporting countries of the Gulf Cooperation Council, the total gross external assets and liabilities of emerging and developing economies continue to grow apace (see also Lane and Milesi-Ferretti 2008). Add to such quantitative data the international expansion of financial intermediaries, where leading investment banks, asset managers, and other service providers (e.g. law and accountancy) have operations in major international and regional financial centers, and "global finance" becomes an even more tangible analytical category (Lee et al. 2009). But how do we make sense of this changing geography of finance?

This chapter provides an analytical frame for explaining financial integration and the convergence of financial practice across different scales and across geopolitical boundaries through a perspective that is interested in both the form of finance, but equally, the functions of finance (cf. Crane et al. 1995; Merton 1995a; Merton and Bodie 2005).[1] It rests on a basic premise that

---

[1] In contrast to the works cited here, function does not necessarily determine institutional form in our perspective. The perspective we adopt in this book allows for functional equivalence among different institutional forms. Form does not necessarily determine function, and function does not necessarily determine form. Nonetheless, like the works cited here, functions provide an important conceptual anchor for analyzing and explaining finance.

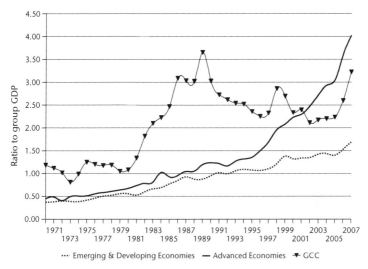

Figure 1.1 Total gross external assets and liabilities, 1970–2007

Source: Updated and extended version of dataset constructed by Lane and Milesi-Ferretti (2007).

financial functions are more stable and vary less across geopolitical boundaries than the institutional form and corporate identities of financial intermediaries. By unpacking form and function, this perspective provides a more dynamic and nuanced means of evaluating and explaining the underlying similarities and convergence processes among geographically distinct financial systems, and their integration with higher scales of aggregation.

This chapter develops this perspective in three sections. The first section, The Functions of Finance, provides an overview of the core functions of the financial system in a market economy. For some readers this section may appear overly elementary. But the point of rehearsing these basic financial functions—notwithstanding the usefulness of doing so for the lay reader in demystifying finance—is to bring to the surface the general significance of taking institutional functions seriously in the comparison of different institutional environments, where institutional forms may be different.[2] The

[2] Although this book is not explicitly about critiquing what is wrong with finance and financial markets (cf. Engelen et al. 2011), it is useful to note that

second section, The Form of Finance, then considers how and why financial systems differ in institutional form from a static perspective. The third section, Integration and Convergence, considers the forces underlying change in financial systems. The final section concludes.

The Functions of Finance

We can delineate five core economic functions of the financial system. These functions are: to provide a payments system to facilitate the exchange of goods and services, to provide a mechanism for the pooling of funds (i.e. the mobilization of savings) to undertake large-scale indivisible enterprise, to provide a means through which economic resources can be transferred through time and across space, to facilitate risk management, and to provide a way of dealing with asymmetric information and incentive problems between the providers (savers) and users (borrowers) of capital.

Facilitating Exchange

We can explain the first function by considering an economy where transactions occur through barter to one where transactions are completed with money. In a barter economy, transaction costs are high because parties to an exchange must evaluate the relative value of both goods against each other. Moreover, each party must be willing to accept the other's goods or services in exchange, which is referred to as a coincidence of wants. Failing a coincidence of wants, there is likely

in taking a functional perspective of finance the analyst can more expressly ask whether the financial system and financial agents and organizations therein are performing their objective economic function (e.g., managing risk or facilitating the transfer of economic resources to where they are most needed).

to be significant limits on the frequency and scope of trade. However, with a medium of exchange (money) used by both counterparties that acts as a measure of value for individual goods and services—also referred to as a unit of account—the problem of comparing the relative value of goods and services directly with each other is unnecessary. The coincidence of wants problem is therefore eliminated. Accordingly, the introduction of money facilitates transactions across a potentially wider range of economic agents.

In increasing the scope of potential counterparties to trade and reducing associated transaction costs, specialization and diversification of economic activity can increase, which are key elements in the process of capital accumulation. Hence, a key role of the state in capitalism, and states in cooperation, has been the establishment of a local currency and payments system, and, in turn, the integration of interstate payment systems wherein one currency can be converted for another (e.g. the Bretton Woods system). If the initial establishment of money increases the demographic scope of exchange, the establishment of a payments system and its further integration with other payments systems increases the potential geographical scope of exchange, thus opening further possibilities of economic specialization and diversification leading to increased capital accumulation. This same logic underlies the rationale behind a currency union (e.g. the Eurozone).

Mobilizing Savings

If establishing a medium of exchange and a system through which that medium can be transferred is necessary for expanding the demographic and geographical scope of exchange and increasing economic specialization and diversification, it is not sufficient on its own. Reaching new markets generally requires new infrastructure such as roads and railways. Increasing the scale of production to meet the needs of those new markets may require the construction of new factories. And both examples may require or engender the development of new technologies. Yet, the challenge of big projects is that they require large sums of capital to complete.

For the most part, few entities or individuals can supply off-hand the required capital necessary to see such big projects to fruition. Conversely, the financial system in a capitalist economy facilitates large-scale projects and the growth of larger and more scale-efficient firms by parceling the total investment needed for a project into small-denomination instruments that are then sold to a large pool of geographically dispersed households, therefore mobilizing their savings. In doing so, the financial system also facilitates the transfer of capital across time and space, thus expanding the geographical scope for potential capital accumulation.

Transferring Resources across Space and Time

But before households and other capital providers relinquish their savings to capital users (e.g. firms, governments, entrepreneurs, and other households) they require information about the viability of the project, as providing capital without such information would be risky (Diamond 1984). They will also want to know more about the capital user. Has the borrower been successful or not in past projects? Does the borrower have the capacity to pay back debts? There is thus a problem of asymmetric information that needs mitigation. For most households acquiring this information would be very time consuming and costly, and they might not have sufficient evaluation skill to judge the viability of a project and the creditworthiness of the capital user.

Acquiring information is even more costly and difficult to judge if those seeking capital are in a different region or country, or if the project is in an area of economic activity that is unfamiliar to potential capital providers. Combined, these factors place a high barrier on the efficient allocation and transfer of economic resources. Yet, because financial intermediaries can acquire information for a large number of potential capital providers and can develop specialist evaluation skills to do so, the cost to each capital provider is significantly reduced through such economies of scale. As a result, capital can be transferred more easily and at lower cost to capital users in different locations, in different industries, and over differing periods of time. Again, this facilitates the demographic and geographical expansion of potential capital accumulation.

Managing Risk

By parceling the total investment of projects, the financial system allows households and/or the institutions that hold assets for households, such as banks and pension funds, to diversify their savings across different projects such that if one investment fails (an idiosyncratic risk) they do not lose all of their capital. Absent the possibility of diversifying across a range of possible investments, capital providers would be less likely in aggregate to part with their accumulated capital, which would subsequently constrain further capital accumulation. This is an important risk management function of the financial system in a capitalist economy.

In addition to reducing idiosyncratic risk by providing possibilities for portfolio diversification, financial markets help reduce liquidity risk. Liquidity pertains to the speed and the ease by which capital providers can convert assets into cash, i.e. purchasing power. For example, a piece of real estate is usually less liquid than publicly listed shares of a major firm; the number of potential buyers of a major firm's shares is normally higher and the costs of completing a trade are much lower. As a result, the shares can be sold more easily and more quickly than can a piece of real estate. But the economic resources of a firm are somewhat just as illiquid as the piece of real estate. Firms are made up of tangible assets such as factories and office buildings, and intangible assets such as intellectual property and production methods. By themselves these assets are normally not very liquid. However, the financial system transforms illiquid production processes and a firm's tangible assets into liquid and tradable financial instruments. Hence, households can provide capital to firms through some type of financial instrument. Yet, because there is a liquid secondary market for these financial instruments, households can convert them into cash if they need to. The same logic holds if households place their accumulated capital with a bank, which provides exposure to a range of intangible and tangible assets through its loan portfolio, while allowing individual households unhindered access to their accounts. In this way, the financial system reduces the liquidity risk faced by investors. By lowering this type of risk, households are more likely to provide capital to illiquid (and potentially long-term) investment projects.

Monitoring and Control

Just as there is a cost to acquiring information on the viability of potential investments, there is a cost associated with ex-post monitoring of capital users. Once capital users have acquired the investment there is no disincentive against capital users misrepresenting the returns of the project or using the funds for something unrelated to the original call for capital (Jensen 2000). Insiders could simply steal the profits made by the firm or they could sell the assets of the firm at below market prices to another firm they control. In the process they would default on their debt or pay no return to outside owners. In effect, there is an asymmetrical insider–outsider relationship to contend with, which distance may further exacerbate. It is in the interests, therefore, of the capital provider to monitor the capital user over the life of the project. However, for the individual investor this is costly. Just as financial intermediaries economize on the costs of ex-ante information acquisition in pooling a larger number of investors, they can also economize on monitoring costs. They can further reduce ex-post monitoring costs by requiring collateral and writing specific financial contracts (e.g. debt contracts) with capital users.

The Form of Finance

Although there are core economic functions common to all financial systems in capitalist economies, the form of financial systems is not always the same. Moreover, there is no one optimal institutional structure for providing these functions to the economy. While global finance has grown substantially, it is still possible to analyze national and regional financial systems. Indeed, inasmuch as capital can flow across geopolitical borders, most households and small and medium-sized firms still acquire capital locally from banks and other financial intermediaries (Pollard 2003). In analyzing the form of a financial system, and specifically at the national and regional level, social scientists generally consider three factors: the institutional form and corporate identity of financial intermediation, the type of legal system and the scope of investor protection, and the sources of liquidity (i.e. the source and depth of potential investment capital).

Banks versus Markets

In the financial system there are two ways capital is transferred between providers and users: direct finance or indirect finance. With direct finance, providers supply capital to users directly. Direct finance can be as simple as friends and family or business angels and venture capitalists providing seed capital to a fledgling entrepreneur. Hence, if you are an entrepreneur it helps to be somewhere where there are large numbers of potential capital providers (e.g. Silicon Valley). However, for entrepreneurs in places without sufficient and willing capital providers, bringing a new business idea to fruition may be more difficult (Klagge and Martin 2005; Martin et al. 2005; Sunley et al. 2005). As such, access to direct finance can vary dramatically from one place to another, which influences how places develop.

With indirect finance there are two mechanisms to transfer capital between providers and users. First, there is the capital market. While it is possible to conceive of the market as a form of direct finance, the point here of considering the market as a form of indirect finance is to acknowledge the very significant role intermediaries play in capital and money market operations. In this respect, the user goes to the market, such as a stock exchange, and raises capital through the issuance of some type of financial instrument (e.g. shares) through the help of intermediaries (a syndicate of investment banks) that underwrite and sell the instrument to capital providers. In this case, providers may be individual households or other financial intermediaries, such as banks, pension funds, mutual funds, and insurance companies, which collect and pool the capital of a large number of geographically dispersed households, acting also as delegated monitors.

For most capital users, however, going to the capital market is not a readily available option. The market—where access is largely concentrated in large financial centers—is usually only an option for large and well-established firms or for firms that demonstrate strong growth potential (e.g. high tech). This leaves most users with the second mechanism in indirect finance, which is accessing capital directly from an intermediary; intermediaries that specialize in this form of intermediation are usually banks. As a result, for most users of capital, access to finance is partly determined by the scope and depth of financial intermediaries in the local vicinity or the penetration of financial intermediaries from elsewhere through other distribution channels (e.g. a credit card issuer). For some users, particularly in poorer or rural areas and even entire countries, financial exclusion can be a significant economic and ultimately social problem (Dymski 2009; Leyshon et al. 2008).

Although these three methods of mobilizing savings and transferring capital from providers to users exist in most financial systems, their relative intensity is generally different across national financial systems (Allen and Gale 2000). Some financial systems have very large and liquid capital markets. The U.S. financial system is a quintessential example. There, firms can access the savings of millions of geographically dispersed households via the country's stock and bond markets, and households can in turn sell their accumulated financial holdings with relative ease to fulfill their liquidity needs. Although most households and small businesses still rely on commercial and retail banks for their financing needs, such large and liquid capital markets in the United States lead some scholars to categorize the institutional form of financial intermediation in the U.S. financial system as market-based.

But not all financial systems have large and liquid capital markets. This is particularly the case for developing economies. Yet, it also has been the case for more advanced economies. For example, in the latter half of the twentieth century national-level financial systems in Western Europe (ex United Kingdom) had what could be categorized as bank-based financial systems (Rajan and Zingales 2003). In Germany, for instance, capital markets were not a major part of how firms raised capital. In contrast, large banks dominated the financial landscape, covering the credit needs of large industrial firms. The large banks were also major shareholders of these firms, which enhanced the banks' monitoring and control capabilities (Deeg 1999). But, as we consider later, financial systems change over time, and the distinction between bank-based versus market-based has become a less tangible descriptor (see also Chapter 4).

Investor Protection

Another way of understanding the institutional form of financial systems is through the legal origins approach, which considers how well outside investors (e.g., the minority shareholders of a firm) are protected (La Porta et al. 1997; La Porta et al. 2000). As such, this approach is interested in understanding the legal rights that define financial contracts and how these contracts are enforced. In effect, this approach is less concerned with the distinction between market-based versus bank-based financial systems. However, geopolitical history and legal origin has shaped institutional forms that may be more or less distinguishable along the market-based versus bank-based spectrum. In this approach, countries are classified into two basic legal families: common law or civil law. Accordingly, the United Kingdom and its former colonies, which include the United States, Canada, Australia, New Zealand, and several countries and territories in Africa and South East Asia (e.g. Singapore), follow a common law system. Common law countries generally have had the strongest protections for outside investors. This has facilitated the development of deeper, more liquid capital markets characterized by geographically dispersed ownership. Not surprisingly, the world's largest financial centers are located in common law countries, or territories that follow common law (e.g. Hong Kong).

Within the civil law tradition, there are more distinctions. French civil law countries, for example, have the weakest protection for outside investors, which historically has constrained capital market development. In these countries, ownership of firms has tended to concentrate in a limited range of owners, typically wealthy families (La Porta et al. 1999). German civil law and Scandinavian countries are in between the common law and French civil law traditions. However, countries in this legal family have strong protection for secured creditors, which historically facilitated the development of more bank-centered financial systems.

Sources of Capital

The sources of capital that fuel the financial system also contribute to its formal development. Without capital providers a financial system cannot exist. A dearth of investable savings is one reason certain low-income economies have underdeveloped financial systems and have relied heavily on foreign capital. For high-income countries, there usually is sufficient capital locally to fuel the financial system. Nonetheless, certain public policy factors have shaped capital accumulation, which in turn have shaped the form of financial systems. For advanced economies, how pension systems developed, especially after the Second World War, helped shape how the country's financial system developed (Clark 2000; Clowes 2000; Drucker 1976). Countries that developed a mix of pre-funded and pay-as-you-go retirement-income arrangements saw the development of large, liquid capital markets. Examples here include the Anglo-American countries and others such as the Netherlands and Switzerland. In these countries, large occupational pension funds accumulated large pools of retirement savings that were then channeled into capital markets, fueling liquid equities and bond markets.

Other advanced economies, such as France and Germany, until recently had pension systems based almost exclusively on a pay-as-you-go model. With the pay-as-you-go model, transfers from current workers are made to retirees. In effect, there is no capital accumulation. The outcome of this policy decision was that capital markets for tradable securities remained relatively underdeveloped in comparison to countries with a greater reliance on pre-funded pensions. Nonetheless, capital accumulation still occurred, as households had high savings rates, which were held as deposits in banks or used to buy annuity insurance products. Hence, these financial systems developed in a slightly different form and fashion from countries more reliant on pre-funded retirement-income arrangements. Yet, this is changing due to pension restructuring (see Chapter 5).

Integration and Convergence

Although it is possible to observe tangible differences from a static perspective in the institutional form of financial systems and the corporate identities of financial intermediaries within them, financial systems and the financial intermediaries that populate them are subject to a range of forces and competitive pressures that alter their form such that tangible differences are muted. These forces and competitive pressures can be divided into three categories: policy convergence, practice convergence, and financial innovation.

Policy Convergence

In terms of the first category, the change of geopolitical borders and the spread of policy and regulatory frameworks across geopolitical borders is a major factor contributing to the change of form in financial systems. A noteworthy contemporary example of this is the European Union. At the heart of the European project is the development of a single market for goods and services, which includes the creation of a single market for financial services (see Lamfalussy 2001). The ultimate goal is to create one coherent financial system in Europe that ensures the most efficient mobilization and allocation of resources across time and space. A key component of this ongoing agenda was the Financial Services Action Plan (FSAP), which lasted from 1999 to the end of 2004.

The FSAP was made up of a set of 42 articles that related to the harmonization of financial services across EU member states that fulfill the objectives of (1) creating a single wholesale financial market; (2) creating an open and secure retail financial market; (3) harmonizing prudential rules and standards of financial supervision. Put simply, the project is about developing new and larger markets; harmonizing investor protection; and expanding the sources of capital available to firms and other economic agents. While tangible differences still exist in the national financial systems among EU member states, European financial integration has made significant progress in the last decade (Grossman and Leblond 2011). It is now much easier for financial intermediaries, particularly at the wholesale level, to operate across borders and for firms to raise capital outside of their home markets. In effect, delineating national financial systems has become more problematic.

At a global scale financial integration is driven through such policy frameworks as the International Financial Reporting Standards (IFRS) developed by the International Accounting Standards Board and the Basel Accords on banking regulation developed by the Basel Committee on Banking Supervision of the Bank for International Settlements. The objectives of IFRS, which have been adopted as the standard in over 100 countries including the whole of the EU, are to provide a common set of financial reporting standards such that investors can easily compare firms on a global basis. This has the consequence of driving the convergence of the financial practices of firms in different countries (see Chapter 6). The underlying goals of the Basel Accords, which are now in their 3rd version, are to harmonize the regulation of capital adequacy and liquidity requirements for banks, which are then implemented through national law. As a result, the Basel Accords help drive convergence of banking regulations across countries, which contributes to the convergence of banking practice.

What is important to understand about policymaking and rules standardization is that it is subject to political contestation and interest group pressure. Policy is never formulated in a political vacuum. For example, the regulatory development of a single market for financial services in the EU has upset the competitive landscape within EU member states, making local financial services providers, such as banks and stock exchanges, subject to greater market forces through the introduction of new outside competition, leading to a reconfiguration of financial center hierarchies (Faulconbridge et al. 2007). Not surprisingly, large globally oriented financial institutions have been key supporters behind the European Commission's efforts to push forward the single market (Mügge 2006).

Practice Convergence

Another complementary driver of financial system change comes from the reduction in barriers to cross-border financial services and the ability of financial services providers to establish subsidiaries in other countries. When major financial services providers establish operations in another country they bring with them particular modes of conduct and potentially different forms of expertise (Knorr-Cetina and Preda 2005). This creates more scope for the convergence of financial practice from one financial system to another. A classic case of such convergence occurred in the United Kingdom in 1986 when the Thatcher government deregulated the London securities market and reduced barriers to foreign entry (Plender 1986). As a result, powerful U.S. investment banks entered the market, upsetting the "private club" mentality of the City, thus creating a more competitive environment. This change was crucial in deciding London's fate as one of the premier international financial centers for the next two decades (Leyshon and Thrift 1997).

In addition to the change dynamics brought through increased competition and multinational market penetration, the education and training of financial professionals is increasingly standardized at a global level, particularly through elite business schools. Such standardization is fostered post-graduation through dense alumni networks, and by the common practice in the financial services industry of sending employees to work for periods of time in different countries (Hall 2008, 2011). Ultimately, these continuous transnational flows of knowledge and people contribute to the erosion of the unique formal qualities of national and regional financial systems.

What is important to recognize about practice convergence is that although common practices become standardized through transnational networks, they originate in particular places that are again subject to specific political, social, and cultural circumstances. For instance, major developments in finance theory over the last half of the twentieth century originated in elite business schools and university economics departments in the United States. Likewise, U.S. and U.K. financial markets have been primary testing grounds for new financial products and practices, which are then disseminated and developed in other financial centers elsewhere. Hence, place is inherent to the development of new financial practices and knowledge creation.

Financial Innovation

Finally, institutional categories have become more arbitrary through financial innovation (Merton 1995b). Such change has been supported in part through advances in computing technology but also through the development of finance theory, which again is spread through transnational knowledge networks. Financial intermediaries are driven to innovate because of competitive pressures and for the demand for better risk management methods. But, as the recent global financial crisis demonstrated, financial innovations do not always lead to positive outcomes in terms of risk management, nor are they always effective at supporting the allocation of economic resources across space and time. Nonetheless, there have been numerous innovations over the last several decades that have expanded the tool kit available to risk managers, investors, and capital users.

What financial innovation has done in particular is to erode the common distinction between different types of financial products. Financial derivatives such as over-the-counter swap contracts allow counterparties to exchange the cash flows of one of the party's financial instrument for those of the other party's financial instrument for a set period of time. Swaps exist for almost any type of financial instrument, from currency to interest rates to equities, and the market for them is global. For example, one party can promise the cash flows from an equity it owns to another party in exchange for a predetermined cash flow from that party. Accordingly, the former party may institutionally hold equities, but in economic effect they now hold debt. If financial intermediaries that have specific corporate identities (e.g. a bank specialized in the provision of debt) can operate in this fashion, then such specific corporate identities become arbitrary and in turn the institutional environment of the financial system becomes more difficult to determine.

Conclusions

There is a reason that finance, financial markets, and financial institutions persist, even after major crises. They emerge to fulfill the needs of exchange, to pool capital for large-scale indivisible enterprise, to transfer resources across space and time, to manage risk and uncertainty, and to deal with asymmetric information problems. The financial system is a core component of any capitalist market economy. Accordingly, understanding the form and functions of finance and financial systems across space and time is part of understanding the uneven and increasingly interconnected geography of capitalism from the local to the global. It has become, however, more difficult to ascertain form, and, moreover, to determine the relevance of institutional form in the face of geopolitical and economic integration across and between scales. Where do the borders of one financial system begin and another start? The challenge, then, is in formulating an effective and dynamic analytical frame for doing so.

In this chapter a simple analytical frame was offered that takes multiple scales into account by considering how financial systems change and practices converge. It was noted that core financial functions in the capitalist market economy change less over time, and that they vary less across geopolitical borders. This allows for an appreciation of functional equivalence among financial systems where the institutional form and the corporate identities of financial intermediaries are different. Moreover, we noted a variety of forces that alter the institutional form and makeup of financial systems such that distinct variety is muted. These forces were delineated into three separate categories: policy convergence, practice convergence, and financial innovation. By unpacking form and function, and the drivers of convergence and integration, we have a more dynamic means of capturing and explaining the changing geography of finance.

2

One World of Production?

For some, the title of this chapter is likely reminiscent of the hyper-globalization theses prevalent in the run-up to the millennium that foretold the end of geography with the progressive dismantling of all sorts of borders, from the cultural to the economic and the political (Fukuyama 1992; O'Brien 1992; Ohmae 1990). The collapse of communism and the inherent expansionary quality of capitalism suggested the beginning of a new political–economic order, one based on an expanded global division of labor, increasing free trade, and the revolution in information and communications technology (Cairncross 1997; Castells 1996). National economies and their distinctive modes of production seemed to be an aging conceptual and material category that reached its apex at the height of the post-Second World War economic reconstruction sometime in the 1960s and 1970s, just as many new nation-states were declaring their independence.

For others the suggestion of one world of production may conjure up a different geopolitical imaginary, one based on Braudel's (1984) *économie-monde*, or world economy. Put simply, world economy delineates a large geographic zone that is subject to capitalist social relations, which may or may not encompass all parts of the globe. Whereas the former hyper-globalist rendering of economic change in the run-up to the millennium suggested the dissolution of borders in the formation of a truly global economy, the latter, articulated furthermore by world-systems analysts such as Wallerstein (2004), emphasized the continual and necessary existence of many geopolitical units that are tied together loosely in an interstate system, and the persistence of cultural and linguistic variety that partly shape everyday patterns of social and economic life. What distinguishes the structure of the capitalist world economy is the division of labor that constitutes it and whose efficacy sustains it. Taking this division of labor to be synonymous with the aggregate production and exchange of goods and services on a world scale, the notion of *one world of production* is not so provocative. One world of production need not signify the end of geography; the social division of labor is not without place (Massey 1984).

Indeed, the social division of labor, separate from the technical division of labor within the firm, is expressed on the one hand by *economic space*, which accounts for the various input–output relationships between firms in a sector or between sectors, and, on the other hand, *geographic space*, which corresponds to the actual location where different parts of the production process take place, from research and development (R&D) to final assembly and distribution. Just as the organizational structure of economic space differs between industries, with some being more centralized around lead producers as in the aerospace and automobile industry, and others being more diffused between small vertically disintegrated producers as in clothing production, geographic space also differs (Scott 2006). Within geographic space is a particular institutional environment that constitutes the informal rules, conventions, habits, and values that shape, condition, and support how producers behave and react to changing economic circumstances (North 1990). More formally, institutions can be expressed through regulations that define such areas as employment relations, corporate governance, vocational training and education, and inter-firm relationships. Institutions are fundamentally about coping with the risk and uncertainty of the market but also the changing conditions of social and economic life more generally.

As the nation-state has often been the key initiator, arbiter, and enforcer in contemporary capitalism of many of these institutions—in the form of regulations and law—and an incubator of social and cultural difference, the geographic space of the social division of labor and the institutional environment therein is frequently expressed and analyzed from the perspective of the nation-state. Hence, under a general rubric of *social systems of production*, there is a large body of literature consisting of a number of different strands—notwithstanding their different theoretical proclivities and empirical foci—that place the nation-state as the preferred unit of analysis. This includes such bodies of literature as the varieties of capitalism approach associated with Hall and Soskice (2001) to Whitley's (1999, 2007) work on national business systems and Lundvall's (1992) work on national innovation systems.[1] As the nation-state is the unit of analysis, capitalism is generally referred to by its national variants (e.g. Chinese capitalism; American capitalism) or by ideal–typical models that are by and large derivatives of country groupings (e.g. coordinated versus liberal versus mixed market economies) (Peck and Zhang 2013). If not explicit, this literature has made a concerted counterargument against hyper-globalization postulates, or those that see the place of the nation-state and nation-state political economy as hollowed out and diminished (Hirst and Thompson 1999). Suggestion of one world of production would seem incongruous with this line of thought.

But much even of this literature has relaxed institutional boundary conditions, allowing for increasing heterogeneity within national political economies and increasing internationalization, which is often synonymous with market liberalization (Deeg and Jackson 2007; Jackson and Deeg 2008). While hyper-globalization theses have been discounted as fanciful if not naive speculation, the increasing integration and growing

---

[1] For other comparable work see: Amable (2003); Berger and Dore (1996); Hollingsworth and Boyer (1997); Kitschelt et al. (1999); Morgan et al. (2005); Sorge (2005); Streeck and Yamamura (2001); Yamamura and Streeck (2003).

interdependence—political and economic—of previously distinctive national political economies continues unabated. Hence, this body of literature, driven in part by historical institutionalist arguments, has begun to focus progressively more on how institutions evolve and change, how institutional complementarities breakdown and decay, and the politics underwriting such processes (Crouch 2005; Hall and Thelen 2009; Streeck and Thelen 2005). Recently, Streeck (2009, 2011) has argued for a return to the study of capitalism as a singular historical social order (see also Blyth 2003; Howell 2003). This, Streeck (2009: 3) argues, is necessary for explaining institutional change in contemporary capitalist political economies, drawing attention to the incentive structures of capitalism and "micro-level dynamics that shape its enactment and reenactment within a specific context of instituted constraints and opportunities."

In economic geography, discussion of multiple varieties of capitalism has not received significant attention in theoretical analysis and empirical verification (see, however, Bathelt and Gertler 2005; Christopherson 2002; Engelen and Grote 2009; Mitchell, 1995; Olds 2001). Conversely, and perhaps due to Marxian and Schumpeterian undercurrents both explicit and implicit, economic geographers have long focused on understanding the functional scope and incentive structures of capitalism as a specific historical social order, while still recognizing *temporary* formal differences in coordinating mechanisms at various scales of aggregation (Dixon 2011, 2012; Peck and Theodore 2007).

While the nation-state remains an important level of analysis in geographical scholarship, the emphasis placed on the growth and decline of regions and cities, and their interconnections, has limited assertive adherence to the study of the institutional environment of production in a strictly nation-state frame (Agnew 1994; Brenner 2004; Taylor 1994, 1995). Such an analytical focus has meant a somewhat different response from economic geography to the changing geography of production and globalization, if generally sharing a comparable but somewhat divergent Ricardian–Listian view of institutionally mediated place-based competitive advantage with the above-mentioned comparative institutionalist literature (Scott 1998; Storper 1997).

Yet, if place-based competitive advantage underpinned by untraded interdependencies reinforces a variegated territorial distribution of production, what role does finance play in underwriting or undercutting such variegation? Much as the notion of "one world of production" may seem hyperbolic, finance and global financial integration provide in many respects the foundation for its realization. Financial flows and processes provide incentives and alternative opportunities to economic actors. If financial systems are converging on a common form whether in the construction of a globally integrated market for financial services or simply through the diffusion and mimesis of particular financial practices, as mentioned in Chapter 1, it is hard to expect continuing divergence in other institutional domains and particular institutional complementarities to persist ad infinitum. Notwithstanding the powerful forces of convergence emanating from global financial integration, modern global finance is in some ways tolerant of institutional variegation. Making a case as such through an approach that is primarily conceptual and theoretical rather than directly empirical, this chapter constructs a perspective on the changing geography of production in relation to the geography of finance.

We consider, in the first instance, the foundations of economic–geographical thought on the territorial logic of capitalism, focusing on the significance of economies of scale and agglomeration. This provides a basis for conceptualizing the changing global geography of production and the driving force of urban and regional agglomerations. The penultimate section, The Scope and Limits of Global Finance, appraises the significance and influence but also the limits of global financial integration, specifically as a vector of institutional change, through the lens of portfolio diversification and liquidity. The Conclusion provides a synthesis of the two lines of discussion.

The Territorial Development of Production

Incessant Expansion

That capitalism is the dominant form of economic organization in most countries today is not surprising given its historical geography. Just as capitalist societies are economically expansionist they tend to be spatially expansionist both within and between distinct political units (e.g. the nation-state). This expansionary tendency is, in the first instance, a product of the technological dynamism of capitalist production, whereby private firms operating under conditions of generalized market exchange and employing wage and salary workers are impelled by competitive forces to generate new products, processes, and inputs (Harvey 1982; Sheppard 2011; Storper and Walker 1989). This expansionary quality is expressed in two forms. On the one hand, spatial expansion results from the ongoing search for, access to, and control over markets for output and sources of material inputs. Throughout the history of capitalism this has been supported at a global scale through military and colonial conquest or diplomatic negotiation (Arrighi 1994; Hobsbawm 1987). On the other hand, spatial expansion results from the appearance of new industries. This occurs regularly in capitalist societies, as a result of technological and process innovation. These new industries, including the reconfiguration and renovation of old industries, may enter new geographic areas and create new centers of growth where none exist, taking advantage of so-called "windows of locational opportunity" (Scott and Storper 1987). However, expansion should not be misread as simply the spreading out of productive activity. At work are powerful economic forces driving the concentration, but also the dispersal of productive activity in its spatial and economic forms (Markusen 1985).

Economies of Scale and Scope

One important expression of economic concentration is the vertically integrated firm, which encompasses a large part if not the entire technical division of labor. Accordingly, a single firm organizes the production process hierarchically from R&D, resource acquisition and assembly, through to marketing and distribution, for example. The firm, in increasing its internal scope, internalizes the markets for each of these activities in a hierarchy of tasks. Consequently, the firm economizes on the transaction costs that would be incurred if external markets were used, such as search-and-match costs associated with finding suitable suppliers, and the costs of drawing up and enforcing the resulting contractual relationship (Coase 1937). Such costs may be considerable in the presence of asymmetric information, where one party has better information than the other and thus more bargaining power, or in the presence of high asset specificity, which is the degree to which a transaction-specific physical or human asset can be redeployed to alternative uses without losing productive value (Williamson 1985). If internalizing more of the technical division of labor concentrates economic activity in a single firm, the pursuit of economies of scale magnifies it: there are incentives for firms to grow in size, whether organically or through mergers and acquisitions, if doing so results in a reduction of the average cost of per unit output, as fixed costs are spread out across more units.

While the relationship is not necessarily causal, economic concentration through the internalization of the technical division of labor and increases in the scale of production within a firm often entails some element of spatial concentration, whether in the form of a single production facility or the co-location of different elements of production in a particular region. In some instances, such as steel production, there are technological reasons for spatial concentration. In other instances, there is a need to locate close to factor inputs, such as large pools of labor in the case of labor-intensive manufacturing. If transport costs are high or if speed is a consideration, there are economic incentives in reducing the distance between elements in the production process and to the markets that are served, or in having easy access to transport networks and infrastructure. Co-location of activities may also be necessary to reduce information asymmetries. For example, if product cycles are short and subject to rapid shifts in consumer demand, there may be reasons for product designers to be located close to the assembly plant, wherein product development becomes an interactive process between those that design the product and those that have to assemble it.

If, however, vertical integration provides coping mechanisms for dealing with risk and uncertainty, the scale of fixed capital and organizational complexity usually involved with vertical integration that build up over time may also concentrate risk. If inertia sets in and the firm is incapable of responding to changing market conditions, then organizational decline and failure may ensue. Such organizational rigidities and sunk costs, or the ex-ante potential thereof, may engender what we can define as economic dispersal, wherein different elements of production are externalized, leading to vertically disintegrated production. The social division of labor is therefore extended in economic space. However, the above-mentioned transaction costs and potential information asymmetries still hold. Hence, in the context of vertically disintegrated production, there are incentives for firms to organize in such a way that reduces transaction costs and information asymmetries, while also allowing for economies of scale.

Economies of Agglomeration

If the transaction costs associated with distance are high, for example, then there is an incentive for firms to cluster geographically. But the potential economic benefits of clustering go well beyond simply the reduction of transport costs. Clustering can produce a range of positive externalities and increasing returns effects, which we refer to as economies of agglomeration, that are beneficial to economic growth and development (Fujita et al. 1999; Marshall 1920). For example, the clustering of firms in related industries produces localization economies that provide scope for the reduction of production costs due to the attraction of larger pools of competing suppliers, and the reduction of overheads and the scale of potential sunk costs at the firm level through the intensification of the social division of labor. Such reductions in cost can materialize through sharing of common infrastructure, and through the increased flexibility provided by multiple suppliers and buyers that react expeditiously to changing resource needs. Accordingly, the flexibility of and access to a dense supplier–buyer network help to mitigate risk and uncertainty for producing firms in rapidly changing contexts and economic conjunctures. Risk is spread across a large number of firms instead of concentrating in one single firm.

As the agglomeration grows and attracts more firms, it also attracts more workers, which, through successive rounds of growth and development, serves to attract more firms (Storper 2011). For firms, access to large diversified labor pools supports productivity growth by reducing search-and-match costs and the risks of costly delays in acquiring the various skill sets they need. For workers, the existence of a large number of potential employers induces them to invest in skills upgrading, particularly if it is difficult to secure long-term contracts, wherein firms are reluctant to make long-term commitments to workers (Monk 2008). The obvious outcome in this case is that risk and uncertainty are transferred to labor. But such risks may be mitigated by the ongoing renewal of productive capabilities in the context of changing market conditions, which are endemic in certain industries. For example, these two factors of access to labor and the capabilities of labor are particularly important for industries subject to rapid shifts in product and process design, such as fashion or consumer electronics, where competitive market advantage usually manifests in temporary actualizations of differentiation. That is to say, these markets are characterized by monopolistic competition (Scott 2006).

The third growth-inducing feature of agglomeration results from innovation and learning effects. Geography is an active constituent in technological innovation and creativity, particularly that related to incremental improvement along the technological frontier (Feldman 1994; Malmberg and Maskell 1999, 2006). Geography is not a passive frame of reference to describe where innovation occurs. Proximity supports the transfer of knowledge—the substance from which new ideas are generated. As a dense network of suppliers and buyers interact through multiple and iterative transactions or explicit collaboration, knowledge spillovers occur that cumulatively reinforce innovation and productive capabilities. Likewise, knowledge spillovers occur through the mechanism of job switching. If specialized workers switch firms, they bring their tacit know-how and knowledge with them (Saxenian 1994). While either of these mechanisms of knowledge spillover can occur at a distance over space, distance entails further transaction costs. The reduction in travel costs and improvements in information and communications technology over the last several decades have removed some of these costs, but only partially (Bathelt and Glückler 2011). Facilitating both mechanisms are socialization and acculturation effects between agents, which geographic proximity helps sustain. As such, innovation and creativity tend to occur in dense agglomerations of economic activity and social interaction.

An Inconstant Geography

Yet, in spite of the benefits of agglomeration, spatial concentration of productive activity can produce a number of negative effects that create strong pressures for spatial dispersal (Scott and Storper 2003). This can occur in the context of both vertically integrated and vertically disintegrated production. Negative effects may include: the costs of urban and regional congestion and pollution; rising land costs or inadequate space suitable for both production and housing; and the potential increase in the bargaining power of workers, and in some cases growing unionization, which places upward pressure on wage costs across firms. Likewise, infrastructure may become outmoded and inefficient for the purposes of production and distribution. Diseconomies of scale may appear, as increases in productive capacity leads to duplication and redundancy; or the introduction of new technologies and organizational schema to the production process is compromised by inherited and unsuitable rules and ingrained social norms (Schoenberger 1997). In all these instances, firms may seek out new locations near or far and/or new activities. The territorial logic of production in capitalism is therefore not constant, but reflects patterns of concentration and dispersal.

Toward a Global Mosaic of Regions

Core and Periphery

Given the tendency toward the economic and geographic centralization of production or particular parts of the production process, coupled with the propensity for its dispersal, the global geography of production historically has been punctuated by core-periphery patterns. The basic formulation of the core-periphery pattern is that higher value-added manufacturing and service activities concentrate and produce core regional agglomerations, which produce goods and services for the local population and export the surplus to other regional centers and to peripheral areas. The periphery on the other hand is distinguished by low value-added agricultural and natural resource production. This distinction between higher and lower value-added production results in varying levels of wealth and prosperity. Hence, the core-periphery model is indicative of wealth disparities between countries at the international level and between regions at the intra-national level (Sheppard 2012).

Throughout much of the twentieth century, largely reflecting patterns established in the nineteenth century and even earlier, the core of the world economy consisted of the industrialized countries of North America, northwest Europe, and Japan, whose economies were driven by national fordist mass-production industries, such as automobiles and domestic appliances, typified by large vertically integrated firms or industrial conglomerates concentrated in core manufacturing regions. National governments provided important coordination and support through national policy frameworks underwritten by Keynesian demand management and expansion of the welfare state (see Chapter 5). Notwithstanding the rapid industrialization of parts of the USSR, the rest, the so-called Third World (now developing nations), remained in relative terms underdeveloped and focused on primary commodity production (Amin 1973).

The End of Atlantic Fordism

By the 1970s, however, the fordist mass-production economy in the industrialized North had lost its foundation. The growth model based on continuous market expansion and increasing economies of scale in production reached a breaking point. Markets became increasingly saturated and consumer demand insufficient to absorb excess production. Competition from process innovations in Japan—only to be reinforced later by the entrance of newly industrialized East Asian economies—unsettled the competitive dynamics of the large industrial firms in the West, sending the leading industrial regions in the advanced capitalist economies, such as the American Midwest or the North of England, into crisis and decline (Bluestone and Harrison 1982; Webber and Rigby 1996). Keynesian demand management was unable to cope with the changing circumstances, and instead produced higher inflation but without growth.

But in the midst of the crisis of fordist mass production in the advanced capitalist economies, new sectors began to emerge based on new forms of flexible and non-routinized production. If standardization and routinization characterized fordism, the new leading edge of capitalist development, based on high-technology manufacturing, consumer-oriented cultural industries, and personal and business services, focused on differentiation, customization, and rapidly changing product designs. The established pattern of industrial geography became furthermore ungirded, as firms in new industries took advantage of new windows of locational opportunity, absorbing different types of urban and regional milieus and clustering to form new industrial spaces in places like Silicon Valley, Baden-Württemberg, or the Third Italy, while the growth in professional and financial services would rekindle growth in large global cities like London and New York (Amin 1994; Amin and Thrift 1994; Cooke and Morgan 1998; Sassen 2001).

A Ricardian–Listian World

Now in the twenty-first century, even if much of this core-periphery pattern at the global scale still holds with large expanses of underdevelopment and economic marginalization within and across countries, the spatial division of labor is increasingly characterized by large specialized industrial agglomerations spread across developed and developing countries. These are connected by increasingly complex commodity chains and global production networks, facilitated by the material removal of political and economic borders and the expansion of transnational corporations that provide important coordination functions (Henderson et al. 2002). While cogent at the time, the predictions of the *new international division of labor* theory offered in the late 1970s that higher-level services and research and development would concentrate in the core (the global North), while lower value-added production is relegated to the periphery (the global South), have not been quite accurate (Fröbel et al. 1980). The rapid export-led development and increasing specialization of previously marginal economies, particularly in East Asia (e.g. Taiwan, Hong Kong, and South Korea), has resulted in new urban growth poles that contain higher-level services and, moreover, are making tangible contributions to technological and process innovation (Saxenian 2006). To paraphrase Scott (1998, 2012), the ensuing geographic structure and driving force of the world economy is not one of national economies, although still an important scale, but rather an interconnected global mosaic of regional economies centered on large megalopolitan city-regions or superclusters. These regional motors of the global economy have large and multifaceted local labor markets with intricate networks of specialized but complementary forms of economic activity. Consequently, each is a nucleus of powerful agglomeration economies and increasing returns effects.

For Scott, the macro-geographic dynamics of the division of labor at these interregional and international scales can be characterized as a Ricardian–Listian world. The reference to David Ricardo captures the effects of competitive advantage through locational specialization. The reference to Friedrich List, who in contrast to Ricardo was an opponent of the absolute doctrine of free trade, captures the political cum institutional mediation of specialization and trade in the course of establishing and sustaining place-specific competitive advantage and regional performance. By melding the two, Scott is confirming the power of competition and markets in ordering economic life and its spatial distribution from the local to the global, while qualifying, on the one hand, that competition and markets do not exist without an underlying framework of institutions and conventions; and, on the other hand, that competition and markets are not without unproblematic effects and failure that require ex-post and ex-ante forms of social and regulatory mitigation (Farole et al. 2011). This also provides further nuance to the dynamics of agglomeration in terms of socially instituted constraints and incentives, which helps explain more clearly why innovation and creativity are endemic in some agglomerations or why certain agglomerations, such as Silicon Valley, continually reaffirm their competitive advantage in the context of technological change and market opportunities (Christopherson et al. 2010; Florida 1995).

This brings us back to our one world of production motif. The Ricardian–Listian view of place-based competitive advantage from the perspective of economic geography affords conceptual scope for spatial distinctions in terms of the places of production—which may very well constitute the nation-state but are more likely to be megalopolitan regions and their hinterlands—and the reasonable expectation that distinctive institutional conditions will be present therein that help shape the capabilities and behavior of economic agents (Gertler 2004; 20114). So, for example, the system of education and training may be apt in producing skilled technicians capable of operating advanced machinery, as the apprenticeship system in Germany is shown to do (Thelen 2004); or there may be a developed venture capital sector that supports entrepreneurship and risk-taking, as in the case of Silicon Valley (Florida and Kenney 1988; Florida and Smith 1993; Zook 2002). However, whatever distinctiveness exists in institutional form and function, such distinctiveness is ultimately subject to the changing imperatives of the market that eventually engender change, whether radical or evolutionary, if such distinctiveness conflicts with those market imperatives. So long as a city, a region, or a national economy is engaged with and part of the global mosaic of capitalist economies, remaining insulated and impervious to changing imperatives is unfeasible. Outmoded forms of production or an inadequate capacity to develop new assets and make use of existing ones, whether in the form of tangible infrastructure or intangible know-how and intellectual property, will eventually be brought to bear by the market. Such is the geographical nature of capitalist market development.

The Scope and Limits of Global Finance

Integration through Diversification

Of the many conventions shaping investor behavior and the scope of the investment universe, the principle of portfolio diversification stands as one of the most significant in terms of its reception and application (Markowitz 1952). At a basic level, portfolio diversification is the most common form of risk management. In investing, there are two basic types of risk: systematic and unsystematic. Systematic risk reflects the general economic and political conjuncture, and hence all securities are affected in some way. It is unavoidable risk. The only way to mitigate systematic risk is through hedging. But as the financial crisis showed, hedging has flaws, particularly when hedging strategies become systematic themselves. Risk is therefore not reduced. As such, systematic risk is often referred to as market risk, aggregate risk, or undiversifiable risk. Changes in interest rates are the most common and most tangible form of systematic risk. In contrast, unsystematic risk is risk that is inherent to a particular firm, industry sector, or country. As unsystematic risk is particular to a single firm or a single industry, wherein the risk of underperformance may vary among firms within an industry sector or among industry sectors, it is diversifiable risk. The underlying rationale of portfolio diversification is to smooth out unsystematic risk in the portfolio such that the positive performance of some securities cancels out the negative performance of others. In its simplest form, then, portfolio diversification seeks to achieve the highest possible return at the lowest level of risk.

While optimal diversification may be possible with a relatively small and well-selected portfolio of securities whose performance is uncorrelated, the pursuit of diversification tends to impel investors to hold very large portfolios of publicly traded securities or other unlisted investments. For large institutional investors, such as pension funds, sovereign wealth funds, or endowments, this is a relatively unproblematic proposition. For small investors, optimal diversification is usually only possible through investment in a pooled investment vehicle, such as a mutual fund, or an exchange-traded fund. Whether the selection of securities or investments is small or large, diversification also tends to drive geographical diversification and expansion. With the progressive removal of barriers to cross-border capital flows over the second half of the twentieth century, the investment universe, and therefore the possibilities for diversification, has grown massively (Sarre 2007).

This does not mean that home bias effects do not exist. Research has shown that investors tend to overweight their portfolios with securities from their home market, even when there are clear benefits to international diversification. There are institutional reasons for this, such as tax effects, but also behavioral reasons such as overconfidence in the ability to pick local securities and greater uncertainty regarding foreign markets (French and Poterba 1991; Wójcik 2011). Nonetheless, how does diversification fit with our conceptual motif of one world of production? From the perspective of the diversified investor, the removal of barriers to international investment to the extent that nearly all markets are potential investment destinations, whether in public or private markets, one world of production is a working reality. Such a diversified global portfolio allows for capture of the value generated from production wherever that may occur or wherever that value is concentrated. Yet this is still a relatively abstract conception of one world of production.

What is important about cross-border capital flows is that it necessarily entails the introduction of external economic agents into national or regional economies that are conditioned by institutional conditions and incentive structures specific to their place of origin. In that respect, cross-border capital flows bring into contact two distinct institutional environments, thus providing a source of institutional change. The larger the size and scope of the cross-border flows the larger, it would seem, is the potential pressure to change. Generally, this pressure to change is associated with investors' performance expectations of investee entities, whether individual firms or entire economies. While investors are looking to minimize portfolio risk through diversification, they are also looking to maximize the risk-adjusted rate of return. Accordingly, for some analysts, the introduction of foreign investors drives firms and other economic agents to focus on shareholder value at the expense of other stakeholders, such as labor, in the local production system (Dore 2008). By this logic, financial integration standardizes the incentive structure facing previously distinct production systems, thus facilitating convergence.

Yet, such institutional change from the removal of barriers to cross-border investment flows need not solely come from external forces. The opening up of the investment universe necessarily alters the foundations on which the local "rules of the game" are set, by providing local economic agents—firms, local investors, or cadres of managers—opportunities for exit or the threat thereof. Any institutional environment has competing claims to authority and resources. Hence, the threat of "global finance" is used as a means for one group of institutional actors in exacting pressure or gaining concessions from another. In other words, local economic agents by actual or threatened defection may force change locally. In this respect, it is not foreign investors that drive the commitment to shareholder value or some other market imperative; rather, it is local agents that are effectuating change. This presumes that local agents hold more decision-making power and influence than do outsiders, as they must ultimately implement a change, whether the impetus comes from within or without (Crouch 2005).

What the growth of global finance implies is that local financial systems are linked in various ways with other financial systems, and that the potential pool of financial intermediaries and forms of financial intermediation is much larger. Accordingly, in a global mosaic of regions, no one region is excluded from the potential influence of exogenous financial agents (e.g. foreign portfolio investors and foreign financial institutions). Finance is the grout that fills the crevices between the pieces of the mosaic, bringing them closer together. Another way in which these exogenous agents in particular and global capital markets in general exert influence as a vector of institutional change is through what we can label the specter of liquidity.

The Specter of Liquidity

According to Keynes (1936), if the *propensity to consume* drives individuals to delay current consumption for future consumption—the *time-preference* for spending now versus saving for tomorrow—there is a subsequent decision on the *form* in which the individual will hold command over future consumption. Does the individual hold liquid command in the form of cash or cash equivalent, which can be used readily as purchasing power? Or does the individual sacrifice immediate command for an indefinite or specified period, leaving it to future market conditions to determine the terms on which the individual can convert savings into purchasing power. Keynes referred to this as the *liquidity preference*. For the purpose of our discussion, the preference for liquidity and the geographical manifestations of liquidity act as a check on the degree to which outside investors are willing to part with their capital in markets near and far.

A market that is highly liquid is a market that is said to be deep. A shallow market is one wherein the speed at which an asset can be converted is slow, or where the costs of doing so are high, meaning that the spread between the bid price and the ask price is wide. The degree of liquidity can refer to an entire market with a range of investment options, such as a national stock market, or it can refer to individual assets and sectors within a market. For example, the securities for large companies are generally more liquid than those for small companies. In times of crisis, triggered by events ranging from natural disasters to political unrest, market liquidity can quickly evaporate. Depending on the size and scope of the event (e.g. a global financial crisis versus a political coup in a small country) the collapse of liquidity may affect many markets and many asset classes, or be confined to a particular market and particular asset classes. In some cases, the collapse of liquidity in one market may drive liquidity in another, as investors shift holdings to more liquid and "safer" markets, often referred to as a "flight to quality." The flight to quality is not, however, a simple unidirectional phenomenon. In the recent global financial crisis, which originated initially in the collapse of subprime mortgages in the United States triggering distress in financial markets around the world, investors piled into U.S. dollar securities. The supposed security and liquidity of U.S. markets meant that investors preferred them as opposed to markets elsewhere, even if those markets had nothing to do with subprime.

There is another element of liquidity that is frequently under-appreciated. While greater turnover of holdings in highly liquid markets suggests a short-term ethic, a market that is highly liquid wherein counterparties to a trade are always available actually points to long-term possibilities. Arguments are often made to the effect that a long-term ethic exists only when turnover is low and holding periods long or indefinite (Dupuy et al. 2010). This ignores, however, that markets and securities that are consistently highly liquid over time suggest that investors have confidence in the long-term prospects of those markets in general and securities therein in particular. There is functional equivalence. To be fair, this does not mean that investors and the firms and governments receiving investment are necessarily focused on long-term issues, such as climate change. Nor does this mean that expectations of performance are not overly focused on the short term. The point, rather, is that realizing long-term objectives ultimately relies on a commitment to concerns ongoing. A high degree of liquidity reflects confidence in those ongoing concerns. Lost liquidity implies a loss in confidence, and in turn the financing of the long-term prospects and possibilities of an economy, an entire sector, or a specific firm.

There are two ways, then, of considering how liquidity shapes local incentives, thus bringing one world of production into reality. Assuming, on the one hand, that most regions of the world over the last several decades have sought foreign capital investment, portfolio and direct, as a way of increasing jobs or bringing in new productive assets and capabilities, attracting such foreign capital usually involves promoting the general liquidity of markets. In promoting the general liquidity of markets, we can include the removal of capital controls, laws protecting minority investors, and the development of local financial infrastructure, such as enhancing local reporting requirements and the information technology necessary to transmit and process such information. By this logic, the local institutional setting is being altered to reflect the expectations of foreign capital, which may be at odds with local tradition or entrenched local interests.

If the initial effort to promote the general liquidity provides an initial jolt to the local institutional environment in terms of introducing the possibility for change, the threat of losing liquidity provides for an ongoing impetus. We can understand this logic by reference to the relative nature of finance in that everything is relative to something else. One investment poses more risk than another. One market is more liquid than another. One country's sovereign debt is riskier than another country's debt. To be sure, certain markets, investment products, and countries are at an advantage to others. U.S. markets, for example, are at an advantage in global markets, given the dollar's position as the global numeraire (Eichengreen 2011). An advanced economy with a strong legal system is at an advantage to a developing economy where the rule of law is weak and recourse to the courts is futile. Among economies at a comparable level of development, those with better investor protection or better relations with capital may have an advantageous position in what is effectively the global hierarchy of liquidity. At times of crisis, as indicated earlier, the relative position in this global hierarchy of liquidity can have significant implications for growth and development, wherein a superior position mitigates the effects of contagion.

Diversity in Diversification

Taken together, the potential endogenous and exogenous forces that result from financial integration provide a powerful driver of institutional convergence. As such, one world of production is less than an abstract category describing the ability of global investors to capture production value wherever it is produced; it is the outcome of financial integration propelling institutional convergence, whether through implicit or explicit mechanisms. But even as the abovementioned forces of convergence loom large, they are in some way at odds with the underlying principle of diversification.

Recall that the point of diversification is to select a portfolio wherein investments are partly uncorrelated such that the positive performance of some investments offsets the negative performance of other investments. If the intensification of economic integration and the convergence of institutional form and function reinforce correlation in aggregate, then the benefits of diversification would diminish. By implication, one world of production is not desirable. This assumes, however, that institutional difference produces a different risk/return profile in the first instance. If that is indeed the case, then it is in the interests of the globally diversified investor for differentiation among geographically distinct political economies to persist. A basic commitment to shareholder value would likely remain, but other institutional variables may be allowed to persevere. Finance driving one world of production does not hold, at least not in a strong form.

We can take the limits of finance as a vector of change further by considering whether finance simply reflects change more generally; in other words, finance follows change instead of driving it. Indeed, for some analysts the role of financial factors in economic growth and development, and the spatial extent thereof, is not seen as significant; finance is simply a sideshow of other more important factors, such as technological or demographic change. Others, in contrast, see a significant and defining role for financial factors. This disparity of views is frequently framed by, on the one hand, the assertion by post-Keynesian economist Robinson (1952) to the effect that where enterprise leads finance follows, compared with, on the other hand, Schumpeter's (1934) argument that financial intermediaries and the functions they provide are fundamental to technological innovation and economic development, as they underwrite the capabilities of entrepreneurs (see Levine 1997). This disparity can be framed in terms of demand-following versus supply-leading finance (Patrick 1966).

Demand-following finance can be described as the process by which financial institutions emerge to meet the demands of investors and savers in the real economy, as it grows and evolves. By this logic, finance is passive to the growth process. The more rapid the growth, the more significant is the demand for finance, as firms are less likely and able to finance expansion from internal funds alone. Likewise, as growth rates vary between sectors, wherein some may be in decline as others are rapidly growing and thus require greater financing needs, the financial system facilitates the transfer of savings from slow-growth to high-growth sectors. In effect, the financial system supports the sectors that are most driving growth. Finance is important, but not central to driving economic growth and development. However, the absence of finance and/or an underdeveloped financial system would likely constrain growth. For example Gerschenkron (1962) argued that it was a lack of modern investment banks that constrained Italy's industrial development in the late nineteenth century. In more recent history, some development economists have argued that rapid financial liberalization in developing economies without sufficiently developed or appropriate legal and regulatory structures may engender financial instability that hinders rather than helps growth (McKinnon 1991; Stiglitz 1989).

Supply-leading finance contrasts with the demand-following form in that financial institutions emerge in advance of demand for their services, assets, and liabilities. The function of a supply-leading financial system is to identify and channel funds to those entrepreneurs and firms that are most likely to implement successfully innovative products and production processes, which underwrite and drive economic growth and development. A supply-leading financial system therefore takes a more active role in distinguishing high-growth sectors, rather than, in contrast to the demand-following finance, simply acting as a conduit through which resources flow from older slow-growth sectors. Hence, the financial system, as a driver of innovation and capital accumulation, takes a more active role in the growth process. In this respect, the financial sector is a real sector in that it researches firms and managers, in addition to providing other functions, such as mechanisms for corporate control, resource mobilization, and risk management. In other words, the financial sector adds value by enhancing *potential* capital accumulation and innovation.[2]

In practice, however, the financial system is likely to contain both supply-leading and demand-following finance. Consider the following sequence. Before growth takes hold, supply-leading finance may induce innovation-type investment. As growth takes hold and growth-leading sectors develop, demand-following finance becomes more significant. Likewise, different sectors are also likely to be at different stages in the sequence. But even as growth takes hold and demand-following finance deepens, supply-leading finance still plays a crucial role in the ongoing identification of growth industries and new growth technologies. Hence, there is an interaction between supply-leading and demand-following finance in driving and sustaining growth. Yet, in both cases there is no guarantee that finance will automatically support growth. Demand-following finance that is poorly developed, and unable to reduce information and transaction costs, could constrain growth. Likewise, supply-leading finance may not accurately identify which technologies and sectors will drive growth. Put another way, the financial services sector, as a real sector, may underperform. The implications are the same no matter the scale of aggregation, from the city-region all the way up to the national level and beyond.

Put simply, financial markets and the institutions and actors that comprise financial markets follow changes emanating from elsewhere, such as technological or demographic change. In other words, financial markets reflect these changes; they are not responsible for these changes. On the other hand, financial markets and the institutions and actors that constitute financial markets drive change. Decisions on the allocation of capital have

---

[2] For a critical discussion on the problematic and contested inclusion of the financial services sector in national accounting statistics see Christophers (2013).

tangible effects. For example, investors may be critical in providing necessary capital for the development of new technologies. Likewise, investors and intermediaries may channel capital away from a city, a region, or an entire economy, on the basis that performance in the future may be poor. As a result, the exit of capital may spur or unnecessarily deepen decline. Just as finance leads change, it also follows. The strength of this measured view on the agency of finance is that it allows ample space for the agency of others, and other structural changes in the economy.

Conclusions

This chapter began by formulating a conceptual motif that in some ways is hyperbolic, depending on how it is interpreted. One world of production in a strong form implies a single global market where barriers to the spatial expression and expansion of production processes are minimal, if they exist at all. Such a view recalls hyper-globalization theses, particularly those of the popular variety (e.g. Friedman 2006). Scholarly accounts of globalization have never quite reached such a fever pitch. While a large body of heterodox political economy scholarship confronted hyper-globalization theses that have been interpreted as denying globalization, the response from economic geography has been a measured one. With a natural inclination to search for and to recognize the contextual significance of particular places as well as the stylized facts of local and regional economies as drivers of capitalist growth at larger scales, but with an appreciation for the instability inherent in capitalism and its expansionary qualities, economic geographers have taken a middle road. Taking the global economy as increasingly capitalist, one world of production is a theoretical possibility. But the economic geography of this world still is not flat (McCann 2008; Rodríguez-Pose and Crescenzi 2008).

While there is no one collective response from economic geography to explain globalization and the spatial structure of the global economy, the chapter builds a view based on the work of Scott (1998, 2012) and his conceptualization of the global economy as a global mosaic of regions. This view considers the spatial and economic organization of firms and the significance of scale and agglomeration economies in driving economic growth and development. This work leaves ample space for local differentiation and local institutional effects in shaping production possibilities and competitive dynamics, while moving beyond methodological nationalism. For Scott, the global economy is structured on Ricardian–Listian competition, where large regions, which may exist in sub-national or international form, compete through specialization that is underwritten by locally specific untraded interdependencies. What is important about this view, however, is that it does not discount the transformative effect of the market in driving change, and thus the possibilities of institutional convergence.

The second half of the chapter was devoted to bringing global financial integration to bear on the structure and scope of the global mosaic of regional economies. On the one hand, an argument was offered that highlights the significance of finance as a conduit of change, providing increased options and incentive for "insiders" and "outsiders" to drive change and ultimately force institutional convergence on previously distinctive institutional settings. This argument was made in abstract terms by referring to demands for liquidity and by the integrative force of diversification strategies. However, this argument was tempered with two points. First, the goal of diversification is to find heterogeneity, as a means of reducing risk in the overall portfolio. Uniformity is not desirable. By this logic, finance is tolerant of institutional variegation and hence regional variegation. Second, while finance drives economic change in some instances, it often follows change. Financial markets may appear to be drivers of change, when actually they simply reflect change emanating from elsewhere. In such cases the agency of finance is weak and therefore likely tolerant of difference, at least in the short term.

This measured view of global financial integration and its transformative effects elides with the conceptual frame of the global economy as a mosaic of regional economies entangled in Ricardian–Listian competition. With or without global finance, the potential for change wrought by global economic integration and market competition is very powerful. Market imperatives must ultimately be addressed, which may result in significant formal change of institutions or at the very least functional change. However, in both cases, difference and differentiation are part and parcel of local competitive advantage on the one hand, and global risk mitigation on the other. This limits the appearance of "one world of production" in a strong form; but "one world of production" in a weak form is not ruled out.

3

Variegated Capitalism and the Firm

A number of interventions have been put forth recently arguing that economic geographers should engage more with recent variants of the varieties of capitalism approach (Hall and Thelen 2009), as part of a reconstituted institutional economic geography (Gertler 2010). Others have suggested furthermore that the varieties of capitalism approach, and its stylization of national political economies as liberal versus coordinated, could be used helpfully in economic geography as a means of generating testable causal theories of political–economic differentiation and the spatial behavior of firms (Engelen and Grote 2009; Engelen et al. 2010). In many respects this is an effort to reinstitute a more balanced view of structure and agency in economic geography in response to the growth and popularity of agency-centered and network approaches in the field (Sunley 2008).

While engagement with broader macro-institutional debates in economic geography is welcome, the challenge of reintroducing a more structural contingency is in determining the spatial extent of structure and as such the causal significance of institutions in a particular territorial setting in shaping the behavior of economic agents, particularly firms (Hess 2004; Jones 2008). Put slightly differently, in a world replete with intensifying cross-border flows of people, capital, and ideas, determining the boundaries of institutions—the formal and informal "rules of the game"—has become increasingly problematic (Jessop et al. 2008). The incentives driving economic actors in some cases may be so strong that they counteract local or national institutional constraints.

At issue, then, is to what extent a reinvigorated institutional economic geography adopts an a priori view of institutions as being hierarchically nested and delimited by specific territorial boundaries (e.g. city, region, and nation-state). Simply including more sub-national layers into an analysis styled on the varieties of capitalism approach does not mollify the problems associated with a reductionist methodological nationalism that obfuscates significant interdependencies, mimesis, and political–economic convergence between countries and other spatial scales. Economic globalization over the last several decades has led firms in some contexts to have more in common and/ or greater linkages with firms in cities and regions in different countries than in their own (Amin 2002, 2004; Phelps 2008). If firms are said to be "embedded," the question must be asked, "embedded" where (cf. Dicken and Malmberg 2001; Dicken and Thrift 1992; Grabher 1993; Maskell 2001)?

For Peck and Theodore (2007) a constructive approach is one that focuses on a nuanced analysis of the temporality and spatiality of uneven capitalist development across political economies. In other words, such an approach does not view "multiple" capitalisms, but views capitalism in the singular, and more importantly as a dynamic polymorphic process whose development is uneven and "variegated." In this respect, capitalist variegation is understood as a more explicitly relational conception of variety, recognizing the strong and complex interdependencies present in global capitalist structuration. By this logic, and keeping with an institutional focus like that of the varieties of capitalism approach, the study of capitalist variegation searches for an institutional theory of capitalism that probes the principles, sources, and dimensions that create capitalist variegation, such as global financial flows pricing inherited traditions of political–economic organization distinguished by geography against market expectations. By moving away from an institutional theory of "varieties of capitalism" to an approach that focuses on understanding variegation *in capitalism*, the tendency to reify institutional differentiation, as the varieties of capitalism literature tends to do, is avoided. In doing so, this approach limits the degree of empirical blind spots, thus producing a better understanding and recognition of systemic interdependence and political–economic convergence occurring across scales, and national and regional economies.

The novelty of Peck and Theodore's variegated capitalism approach is that it utilizes long-standing tools and practices of economic geography; in this respect it is actually not particularly new. Simply stated, the approach suggests that the work done by economic geographers in the 1980s on uneven spatial development (e.g. Massey 1984) should be conjoined with later institutionalist economic geography work on factors endogenous to local and regional economies (see e.g. Feldman 1994; Gertler 1995; Peck 1996).[1] The latter, although rich in empirical detail and understanding of local governance, has had a limited amount to say about broader macro-institutional configurations or inter-local and international "rules of the game." Combining the two traditions achieves a more concerted capacity to engage with broader macro-institutional comparative political economy debates.

Problematically, however, Peck and Theodore's variegated capitalism approach remains largely silent on a theory of the firm and where exactly the firm should be placed in the analysis. Although such partial obfuscation of the firm is not a problem when attempting to "know" capitalism and capitalist processes from a more holistic perspective, such holism and pluralism are likely to limit the capacity of a variegated capitalism approach to effectively engage with the varieties of capitalism approach, as the latter places the firm at the center of the theory and at the

---

[1] See Scott (2000) for an overview on research trajectories in economic geography during this period.

center of nationally differentiated macro-institutional spaces. Accordingly, effective theoretical engagement with varieties of capitalism necessarily requires an explicit consideration of the firm. This is not to imply that a firm-focused approach ignores other institutional domains. Indeed, understanding the firm—its capabilities, its decision-making, and its location strategies—necessarily requires an analysis of a multitude of institutional spheres, from the financial system and industrial relations, to inter-firm and state/firm relations.

The next two sections, Varieties of Capitalism, and Variegated Capitalism, review the core propositions of the varieties of capitalism approach in conjunction with a presentation and reformulation of Peck and Theodore's critique. I extend this critique by reconsidering the status of institutions and the relationship between form and function, arguing that institutional function does not necessarily follow institutional form. This allows for a greater appreciation of functional equivalence, wherein institutions of ostensibly different forms produce analogous functions. What is significant about this argument is that it brings to the surface institutional convergence that remains hidden behind an unchanging institutional form. The penultimate section, Firms in a Global Economy, turns our attention to the firm and the difficulties in locating its identity, arguing that if firms in previous periods of capitalist history were held hostage by their history and geography, global financial integration coupled with the globalization of supply chains through outsourcing and offshoring has liberated them. The final section concludes.

Varieties of Capitalism

In the varieties of capitalism approach firms are seen as the key loci of a national institutional constellation, whose qualities of economic adjustment are conditioned by the relational logics between the various components: other firms and producer groups, employees and trade unions, and sources of financing.

The quality of these relationships depends crucially, in turn, on the degree of support conferred by political coalitions. National political economies are represented as having distinct institutional ecologies, where firms' strategies are conditioned by the functional complementarities of the relationships among multiple institutions. Institutional ecologies are categorized by means of two ideal types: the coordinated market economy and the liberal market economy (Hall and Soskice 2001; see also Hancké et al. 2007).

In the ideal–typical coordinated market economy, non-market forms of coordination dominate convention. Industrial relations are distinguished by formal or informal coordination of wage determination across key industries, with employer associations and trade unions playing decisive roles in wage determination at the national level. At the level of the firm, employee-elected bodies such as works councils, and membership of employees on corporate boards, ensure that employees are involved in firm-level decision-making. In contrast, wage bargaining in the ideal–typical liberal market economy, where market-based relationships dominate convention, occurs at the level of the firm. Trade unions have limited involvement at the workplace, and wages are determined by general conditions in the labor market. In the ideal–typical coordinated market economy, firms are involved significantly in vocational training regimes, thus tying employees to firms for the long term. In the ideal–typical liberal market economy, firm-supported vocational training is weak but post-compulsory higher education is stronger (Busemeyer and Trampusch 2012).

In the ideal–typical coordinated market economy, inter-firm relationships are close, with standard setting based on consensus. Technology development is institutionalized in close relations between business associations and educational institutions. Domestic competition is kept to a minimum, but is open in export markets. In the ideal–typical liberal market economy, standard setting is left to the market; strong anti-collusion policies prevent non-market coordination; and technology diffusion is not institutionalized.

In terms of financing, banks play a strong monitoring role in the ideal–typical coordinated market economy, where firms benefit from stable shareholder arrangements, higher levels of loan financing, and legal limits to hostile takeovers. Capital is considered "patient" (Goyer 2011). This feature, in theory, allows firms to make investments on a longer time scale. Corporate finance in the ideal–typical liberal market economy is based on unstable shareholder arrangements and significant equity financing, which induce firms to make short-term profit-maximizing investments. Hostile takeovers are permitted and common, which has consequences for the capital investment horizon of firms, leading to the realization of fewer sunk costs and a preference for interchangeable investments (Vitols 2005).

In theory, these different institutional environments are associated with distinct economic outcomes, at both micro- and macro-levels, which influence different production strategies, forms of innovation, and the degree of inequality in society. Put slightly differently, complementarities reinforce national equilibria that give rise to comparative institutional advantage in particular areas of production. For instance, coordinated market economies are associated with incremental innovation that requires significant investment lead times and sunk costs. Liberal market economies, in contrast, are associated with more radical innovation (e.g. software development) that requires limited fixed capital. Likewise, because of the strong institutionalization of labor relations and social protection, wage inequality is kept to a minimum in coordinated market economies. In liberal market economies, social protection is weaker and skills are not "firm-specific," which leads to higher wage inequality (Pontusson 2005). By default, the approach conveys a world of competing capitalisms (Albert 1991).

These institutional environments, distinguishable by the degree of non-market to market-based coordination, are held to be relatively static in their composition; they are path-dependent systems. The varieties of capitalism approach presumes, therefore, that a firm in a coordinated market economy will be unlikely to withdraw from institutional relationships bound by non-market coordination, as the costs of doing so outweigh the potential benefits. The varieties of capitalism approach rests, then, on an assumption that more coordinated political economies are unlikely to converge toward more liberalized modes of capitalism due to increasing returns to scale; or put another way, due to sunk costs.[2] In other words, the embeddedness of particular modes of coordination are to a degree whereby abandonment of such modes of coordination in the face of changing conditions, namely global competition and economic integration, is precluded.

Variegated Capitalism

Beyond Methodological Nationalism

It is partly the methodological nationalism and "container model" of economic systems that leaves the varieties of capitalism approach open to so much scrutiny from an economic geography perspective. Whereas varieties of capitalism scholars regularly and uncritically accept the national scale as given as the primary locus of economic activity/organization, economic geographers problematize spatial variegation across multiple registers (see Table 3.1). Indeed, Peck and Theodore (2007: 759) in their critique emphasize that in economic geography, "the spaces and scales that are constructed by circuits of value and regimes of valuation are no longer assumed to be pregiven." This is due to economic geography's focus on the sub-national scales or global transnational networks, in

---

[2] Sunk costs correspond to a non-recoverable commitment to production in an industry. Sunk costs can be disaggregated into three different types: setup sunk costs (initial capital investment); accumulated sunk costs (normal costs of doing business); and exit sunk costs (such as early-retirement pension entitlements or plant decommissioning costs).

Table 3.1 Varieties of capitalism versus variegated capitalism

	Varieties of capitalism	Variegated capitalism
Problematique	Understanding institutional variability among advanced capitalist economies	Explicating processes and forms of uneven development within, and beyond, late capitalism
Case study rationale	Comparative cases positioned relative to the privileged axis of LME ⟷ CME	Individual cases selected according to their theoretically generative properties
Method	Tendency for parsimonious institutional political economy with strong rational-choice component; ideal-typical theorizing; reliance on secondary sources and game-theoretic procedures	Relatively ecumenical institutional/cultural political economy, elaborated through qualitative case studies; post-positivist theorizing; inclination to urban and regional analysis; rejection of methodological individualism
Privileged agents	Firms, business associations, and policy entrepreneurs	Agents generally afforded relatively weak analytical status, as bearers of prevailing modes of restructuring or nascent forms of resistance; agents embedded in constitutive network relations
Analytical gaze	Privileging of national institutional archetypes and relatively bounded national economies; emphasis on lead firms, dominant industries, and formal institutions	Emphasis on decisive moments of economic transformation and institutional restructuring; real-time analysis of regulatory projects and experiments in the organization of production; multi-scalarity
Form and function	Institutional function follows from institutional form	Institutional function does not necessarily follow from institutional form; different institutional forms can have equivalent or near-equivalent functions
Temporal dynamics	Presumption of equilibrium within selected institutional fields (absent exogenous shocks); emphasis on relative stability, incremental change reinforcing institutional settlements, punctuated by occasional disruptions	Dynamic analysis, concern with endemic restructuring; presumption of disequilibrium and persistent crisis-proneness

(Continued)

Table 3.1 (Continued)

	Varieties of capitalism	Variegated capitalism
Scalar dynamics	Methodological nationalism; presumption of high degrees of endogenous institutional coherence and a unified national-economic space; supermodularity registered at the national scale	Social construction and relativization of scale; potential for supermodularity and conjunctural effects at multiple spatial scales (e.g. "locality effects"); concern with multi-scalarity (e.g. "glocal" hybrids and cross-scalar networks)
Historical trajectory	Dual convergence or "twin peaks"; static-comparative analysis of archetypal development models	Combined and uneven development; embrace of contingency; rejection of the necessity of either convergence or divergence; concern with path-shaping and path-altering change
Typical levels of abstraction	Micro-analytic accounts of firm behavior embedded within meso-level institutional architectures	Meso-analytic interpretations of relatively concrete institutional conjunctures located within unevenly developed (capitalist) system
Normative project	Defense of European- and Japanese-style social democracy and corporatist regimes; concern to explicate non-neoliberal modes of development	Revealing internal contradictions of neoliberal globalization; identification and promotion of alternative (and/or progressive) forms of local development

Source: Adapted and extended version of Peck and Theodore (2007), table 3.

comparison to varieties of capitalism scholars' big-picture focus on multiple institutional domains along national lines. Put slightly differently, economic geography's roots in understanding local and regional phenomena has meant that the national scale has been only one of many scales, whereas the varieties of capitalism approach's roots in comparative politics has meant that the national level has been the prime scale of focus. Yet in a demonstrable world of continually ongoing multi-scalar capitalist economic activity and transformations crisscrossing and connecting multiple distinct institutional configurations, a national-level comparative focus results in innumerable empirical blind spots, thus leading to an unstable and temporally untenable theory.

As discussed, a variegated capitalism approach does not uncritically begin analysis necessarily from the national scale. More importantly, however, a variegated capitalism approach is explicitly concerned with conjunctural effects and how one agent's decision affects the incentives of others, i.e. supermodularity, at multiple spatial scales. This contrasts sharply with the varieties of capitalism contention that significant levels of endogenous institutional coherence exist in the national–economic space. In the variegated capitalism approach, a strong institutional coherence may exist at the national scale, but it is not necessarily presumed. Moreover, the approach is not satisfied with demonstrating national-level institutional coherence alone, but rather understanding and finding the various multi-scalar relationships extant above and below the national scale that fit into a larger whole (i.e. global capitalism/regionalism). For instance, many coordinated market economies (e.g. Germany) are major exporting economies that ship their wares to liberal market economies and emerging market economies (e.g. China and India). That coordinated market economies depend so heavily on their economic growth from demand from different institutional configurations poses an interesting theoretical question for the so-called "coherence" of the domestic institutional environment.

There is a need, therefore, to understand variety in relational terms—something economic geographers have increasingly argued for (Bathelt and Glückler 2003; Hess 2004; Yeung 2005). Hence, a variegated capitalism approach also resonates with the work on global production networks (e.g. Coe et al. 2008; Henderson et al. 2002; Hess and Yeung 2006); evolutionary approaches to economic geography (Boschma and Frenken 2006; Boschma and Martin 2010); and broader efforts to aggregate spatial categories (i.e. territory, place, scale, network) in order to understand polymorphous socio-spatial processes in contemporary capitalism (Brenner 2003; Jessop et al. 2008).

Methodological nationalism also makes it difficult for the varieties of capitalism approach not to move away from more simplified convergence/divergence debates, such as those over degrees of neoliberalization of political economies (Brenner et al. 2010). In utilizing the liberal versus coordinated market economy distinction, the varieties of capitalism approach attempts to disprove neoclassical convergence theories, noting significant diversity among political economies. However, in doing so, the approach almost by design leads to a "twin peaks" or "dual convergence" thesis (see Hay 2004). The shift recently to a more historical–political approach across the literature has helped move the approach slightly away from more simplified forms of the debate, yet the focus on comparisons between groups of families of national political economies at either end of the liberal market versus coordinated market economy spectrum, or simply the preference for national-scale analysis, precludes the approach from conveying a more multidimensional understanding of convergence and divergence (Djelic and Quack 2010). The variegated capitalism approach, in contrast, avoids the debate altogether. This is largely based on its core premises of multi-scalarity and *capitalism* in the singular. Capitalist development is inherently uneven; as such, there is not a single common trajectory nor is there a common end point.

Beyond Path Dependence

This relates to another important difference between the two approaches: equilibrium versus disequilibrium. In the varieties of capitalism approach, institutional constellations are calculated in a game-theoretic fashion in terms of punctuated equilibrium, with an emphasis on stability. The variegated capitalism approach, in contrast, presumes disequilibrium, endemic restructuring, and crisis proneness. Such presumptions characterize much of economic geographic theory and research. So, for instance, although a "national" institutional configuration may appear to be in equilibrium and relatively coherent, it is still likely part of larger processes that are not in equilibrium or have disequilibria at sub-national scales that ultimately affect the supposed institutional equilibrium at the national level. With the presumption that multiple disequilibria exist combined with a multi-scalar perspective, the variegated capitalism approach is thus more apt to reveal and understand such important spatial constructions and their effects.

Whereas the varieties of capitalism approach has been more explicit about arguing the existence of path dependence limiting the radical or accumulative transformation of distinct national political economies, and the potential for convergence to more liberalized Anglo-American forms of corporate and political–economic behavior, the concept of path dependence in economic geography has had a more problematic uptake. Martin and Sunley (2006) have argued that path dependency can be a useful concept for explicating differentiation of the economic landscape, but they seem relatively uneasy about its salience over the long term, as the potential for path creation and the capacity to break free of old "locked-in" traditions and trajectories are equally important. As Martin and Sunley (2006: 428) note, "path dependence, we suspect, has tended to over-emphasize the replication function of economic reproduction mechanisms and to downplay their simultaneous innovative role." In essence, path dependencies exist, yet it is highly problematic to assume that they are frozen and that radical change is impossible.

Neo-Marxian economic geographers working on uneven development in the 1980s likewise argued that the economic landscape oscillates between fixity and flux. In other words, the spatial configuration of economic activity is periodically disrupted by the introduction of new technology and by shifts in the mode, organization, and profitability of production (see e.g. Harvey 1982). On the one hand, such work suggests a particular degree of path dependence, but such path dependence is ultimately trumped by always impending crisis. As Massey's (1984) work suggests, remnants of the past coexist and help shape the constitution and location of the new. The co-constitution of the economic landscape with both old and new is important, suggesting that overemphasizing the old, that is, assuming continuing fixity and path dependence of a particular institutional regime, may obfuscate the potentially powerful change brought by the new, which ultimately may counteract and replace previously important elements of the old.

History and geography matter, but change is inevitable, as the future, unlike the past, is uncertain. It is in this uncertainty that the past may not necessarily shape the outcomes of the future, particularly as the spatial extent of that future is likely to be radically different from the past (e.g. contemporary economic globalization). Hence, as Thrift (2005: 4) states,

> capitalist firms may be able to mobilize power and enrol allies but they are as uncertain about the future as we all are because the future unfolds as a virtuality—it is continually creating temporary actualizations out of new questions—not a known quantity, or at least a distinct possibility. So capitalist firms may sit on the bridge of the world, able at their best attempts to steer it in certain directions, but they still cannot know what is around the corner.

Function before Form

If Peck and Theodore's variegated capitalism offers a useful frame for a reinvigorated institutional economic geography, it would also need to reframe the relationship between form (e.g. public versus private) and function. The varieties of capitalism approach presumes that function follows from form. Framed in this way there is a larger probability of overemphasizing the differentiation of institutional form, while discounting potentially significant similarities in the function of institutions across political economies such that the "rules of the game" of one particular institutional setting appear more idiosyncratic and are ascribed greater explanatory power on the behavior of economic actors than is warranted. As Rodríguez-Pose and Storper (2006: 5–6) note, the typological comparisons of institutional form at the heart of the varieties of capitalism approach, and those of complementary approaches, are "limited in their ability to determine whether institutions that appear different are somehow similar in some deeper underlying way." They contend furthermore that the coordinated versus liberal market economy dichotomy does not adequately capture the underlying forces of coordination, as the functions of coordination may take on different institutional forms in different places.

At the same time, placing form before function excludes the possibility that the sequencing and speed of change is different for institutional functions than it is for institutional forms, wherein ongoing divergence of institutional form can mask significant institutional convergence. Again, this is particularly relevant in that global economic integration and interdependency means that the agency of firms may be driven more by common capitalist market imperatives, namely competition, than distinctive local "rules of the game," particularly over the long term (Dixon and Monk 2009; Monk 2009a).

How then should institutions and institutional change be treated? For Clark and Wójcik (2007: 8) "institutions are created in response to market imperatives, those imperatives continue to evolve (or dissipate) so as to (in part) reinforce those institutions but also, inevitably, undercut their longevity." In other words, institutions may be inherited but they must necessarily adapt to meet changing market imperatives if they are to remain viable and effective. The form of an institution may appear different in respect to other capitalist economies, but its function drives toward the functional mean demanded of current capitalist market imperatives. And as changing the functions of institutions need not necessarily require significant change to the form of institutions, the form of institutions and the identities of those economic agents that mediate those institutions may continue to diverge while the functions of institutions converge (or are in the process of converging).

What this perspective of institutions and institutional change does is take a middle ground between the functionalist-leaning view of economic processes characteristic of neoclassical economics and the institutionalist perspective that views economic processes as partly determined by social, cultural, and political conditions. What it also does is take seriously the hegemony of capitalism and its ability to innovate and reproduce itself in the face of changing geopolitical and technological conditions. By breaking the distinction that function follows from form, this perspective of institutions and institutional change avoids the potential pitfalls of methodological territorialism, which tends to hold history and geography static, while eschewing a post-structuralist view of agency. As such, it provides a clearer view of the forces of economic integration and mimesis that are changing previously distinctive economic geographies across different scales. This is particularly apposite in a world where the globalization of finance and the globalization of supply chains unshackle firms from the weight of history and geography.

Firms in a Global Economy

Hostage to History and Geography?

The main task of firm decision-makers, which is primarily management, is to manage the inherited spatial and functional configuration of the firm's capital in order to realize the value of the firm as a functioning economic entity. Management, depending on context, may experience different degrees of contestation on the part of shareholders and other stakeholders, but it is ultimately tasked with effectively mobilizing disparate and often conflicting stakeholders (themselves included) in order to face current industry competition. The firm is therefore not a fixed object but an entity that is always in the process of becoming. This can be a process of becoming obsolete or a process of becoming a highly efficient and competitive producer, and anywhere in between. In this process of becoming, different resources (such as labor or sources of capital) may be mobilized, reallocated, restructured, or even discarded, depending on the needs of value realization. In no way can the organization of the firm, and thus its relations with complementary institutions (e.g. labor, finance, and the state) be assumed to be ideal or fixed, at least over time (Taylor and Oinas 2006).

To paraphrase Schoenberger (1997, 2000), firms are in the process of (or in constant struggle with) validating spatiotemporal processes in order to remain a viable going concern. Hence, the competitiveness of a firm is not simply a function of prices, products, and market entry considerations, but crucially the management of time and space. As spatiotemporal processes are necessarily social, they are part of a whole gamut of social relations, whether conflictual, competitive, or cooperative, which themselves are historically contingent and subject to competing visions of the rightness and productiveness of different spatiotemporal models (and arguably at changing spatial scales). This, Schoenberger (2000: 330) emphasizes, "guarantees change in general, but what kind of change and who will fight for it and who will resist depends on particular historical–geographical conditions."

In their account of sunk costs, Clark and Wrigley (1997a, 1997b) argue that firms are complex organizations that are less than ideal in structure, decision-making, and performance; they are unable to adjust without cost to changes in market demand and prices; and they operate in a world of imperfect competition. Given sunk costs, firms are ostensibly held hostage by their histories and geographies. Change is difficult and does not occur seamlessly. It may seem relatively easy to assume in this case that a firm will conform to a particular path, even if such a path is ultimately unsustainable given evolving market conditions and competitive pressures. This narrative may have been accurate for the industrial firm of the 1970s and 1980s, but the globalization of production and the globalization of finance have served to liberate firms from their histories and geographies.

Outsourcing, Offshoring, and Global Finance

If trade in primary commodities and finished goods domi-nated international trade in previous periods of capitalist his-tory, the contemporary growth and expansion of global supply chains and global production networks, made up of an assem-blage of firms large and small extended across many geopoliti-cal boundaries, has altered radically the form and function of international and interregional trade (Grossman and Helpman 2005; Grossman and Rossi-Hansberg 2008). The tasks associ-ated with the production of complex industrial goods such as automobiles, airplanes, and microelectronics occur in a range of different countries and regions, and across a range of differ-ent firms. Even less complex goods, such as children's toys, are likely to be designed, produced, assembled, and assessed for quality in production networks that span different countries. But the outsourcing of different tasks to different suppliers and the corresponding offshoring to different countries and regions is not exclusive to manufactured products. With the revolution in information and communication technologies of the last two decades and the growth of passenger aviation, business and con-sumer services also have been increasingly subject to outsourc-ing and offshoring (Bryson et al. 2004).

If part of the impulse underlying offshoring and outsourcing has been to reduce labor costs or to find preferential regulatory environments, it is also about gaining access to new markets and specialized regional agglomerations where specific exper-tise and powerful externalities are at work, as mentioned in Chapter 2. Notwithstanding the enduring place of local "rules of the game," this change in the form and function of inter-national trade in goods and services has reconfigured the scale and the spatial context of the structural influences facing the firm. Put simply, the agency of firms is influenced by a regional or national institutional environment but also the institutional effects derivative of the relationships and iterative interactions with external agents in global production networks and other regional agglomerations (Bathelt and Glückler 2011). As such, it is difficult to pinpoint a firm's loyalty (in a national sense) and the local institutional factors that determine its behavior. Firms may utilize particular institutional settings to their strategic advantage, such as one where labor relations are stable and conducive to ensuring a skilled workforce. Yet, with the ability to relocate production and reassemble supply chains, firms are not bound indefinitely by the institutional relationships of any particular institutional environment.

The growing extent of foreign ownership of public equities in the advanced economies since the early 1990s puts this growing independence in further relief. Figure 3.1 illustrates this point

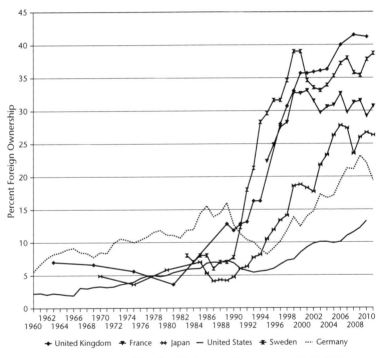

Figure 3.1 Foreign ownership of publicly traded companies, 1960–2011

Source: Federal Reserve Statistical Release, Z.1, Flow of Funds Accounts of the United States; Deutsches Aktieninstitut Factbook 2010; UK Office for National Statistics, Share Ownership Survey, 2010; Tokyo Stock Exchange, Share Ownership Survey 2011; Statistics Sweden, Shareholders Statistics; Banque de France, National Financial Accounts.

by showing the percentage of total foreign ownership of publicly traded companies for five high-income economies. For the United Kingdom, France, Sweden, and Japan, foreign ownership exceeds 25 percent. In Germany, foreign ownership accounts for roughly 20 percent of share ownership. The United States, the lowest of the group, has less than 15 percent foreign ownership. However, as these are aggregate numbers, they do not account for those firms where foreign ownership exceeds that of local ownership. For example, foreign ownership of Siemens, the largest German multinational by market capitalization, was 70 percent at year-end 2012. Foreign ownership of Sanofi, the largest French multinational by market capitalization, was 65.5 percent at year end 2012.[3]

Underwriting the growth in foreign ownership, particularly in places like Japan and Europe, has been growing convergence in the form and function of corporate governance regimes. If foreign investors, particularly large institutional investors from the Anglo-American world, brought with them certain expectations surrounding corporate performance and transparency, governments obliged these requests through regulatory reform, undermining local traditions of corporate governance in the process (Harmes 1998). Management and other large legacy owners took advantage of the new environment to strengthen their power vis-à-vis other stakeholders, particularly labor (Johal and Leaver 2007). Remnants of past tradition persist, such as trade union representation on company boards, but their influence is not what it was. Hence, diversity among corporate governance regimes persists, and convergence to a singular model seems unlikely.

The wider picture is, still, one where the stakeholder model of corporate governance—wherein a wider constituency including employees and the local community has a claim to the value generated by the firm and to how the firm is governed—has been weakened and increasingly supplanted by a shareholder model

---

[3] Data for Siemens and Sanofi are based on company reported information.

of corporate governance, in which shareholders, as owners of the firm, have an overriding claim to the value generated by the firm (Barker 2010). This does not mean, though, that shareholders are actually the main beneficiaries. For some, the shareholder value revolution has benefited primarily the managers of firms at the expense of shareholders as well as labor and the wider community (Froud et al. 2006; Stout 2012).[4]

In most countries, however, large global firms are few in comparison to small and medium-sized firms in terms of numbers and overall employment. For most of these firms the workforce and operations are local, as is ownership. In this case it would seem unproblematic to denote identity by recourse to a specific geopolitical location. By extension, one may infer that the spatial context of the incentive structure that shapes the agency of the firm is specific to that geopolitical location. An export focus or being in the service of export-focused industries need not necessarily alter this situation. The local institutional environment may actually be to the advantage of such firms. However, while the local institutional environment is likely to engender certain behavior, and even demand particular modes of conduct in the case of specific regulations, integration with the wider global economy brings its own incentives. Although less ambiguous and problematic than the case of the large global firm, classifying the agency of smaller globally oriented firms by recourse to national origin and context has limits.

Conclusions

Notwithstanding systemic shocks such as war or financial crisis, the outlook of capitalist firms is and has been global (Dunning 1993; Jones 2005; Vernon 1971). A possible retort to this

---

[4] Convergence on particular organizational structures (e.g. the multi-divisional form) is likewise significant, yet does not form part of our discussion here (see Whittington and Mayer 2000).

assertion is that most firms are small and only serve local markets and local needs, and therefore their outlook is not global. A rejoinder to this counterclaim is that even ostensibly local firms support other smaller or larger firms that seek to serve extra-local markets, if only indirectly by supporting the needs of the local economy and the local workforce. For small open economies this is especially apposite. As observed in Chapter 2, the geographical extent of the global economy has been different; markets, potential or otherwise, have been out of reach for a whole range of reasons, from the limits of communications technology and transport capabilities to political (and sometimes cultural) boundaries. Yet, in the long run, such limitations have been temporary at best. In the contemporary period, few places are without reach. Capitalist firms eventually adapt to any social context, if the social context has not already to them.

The quintessential expression of this global projection is the multinational enterprise, or as it is quite frequently referred to, the transnational enterprise. Such a semantic difference is not trivial, however. Multinational suggests parentage or belonging to a specific set of nation-states. Transnational implies a firm that transcends any particular nation-state. In that most large global firms find their origins and headquarters in the developed economies of North America, Europe, and East Asia, coupled with at least implicit support by particular national governments for their activities on the global stage through, for example, trade promotion and the protection of intellectual property rights, the multinational signifier seems logical. But considering the global reach and size of many large corporations, many of whom have annual revenues that surpass the gross domestic product of many small developing countries, the transnational signifier also appears logical. In either case, identifying a large global firm by recourse to a specific geographic location, such as the nation-state, is problematic.

While firms are shaped by the institutional environments in which they originate and operate, with some residing in more cooperative environments than others, the empirical record continues to show divergence from such trends. History and geography matter, but history is constantly in the making and the future is laden with uncertainty. The varieties of capitalism approach has been useful in explicating the constitution of coordinated market economies, particularly Germany, as they stood in the early 1990s. However, more than two decades of intense economic, financial, and political globalization has reshaped the history from which firms and their complementary institutional relations will go forward. The relatively short history of industrial capitalism, as contrasted with human history, has changed radically from the factories of northern England in the nineteenth century to the vast global production networks of today. Adding the powerful dynamic of global financial integration to the mix furthermore challenges our ability to hold the story of capitalism as experienced in any one location fixed for any considerable period of time necessary for the development of political–economic theory.

4

Comparing Financial Systems in a Global Economy

As the global financial crisis wreaked havoc across many parts of the global economy, the media were awash with voices proclaiming the end of unfettered *Anglo-Saxon* financial capitalism. Leaders in continental Europe, particularly French President Nicolas Sarkozy and German Chancellor Angela Merkel, called for a reformulation of global capitalism along models of capitalism espoused in Europe. Nicolas Sarkozy proclaimed in one speech, for instance, "the crisis was a product of the Anglo-Saxon model; I want for the world the victory of the European model, which has nothing to do with the excesses of financial capitalism."[1] Merkel, likewise, in a speech to the World Economic Forum, proclaimed that the social market economy is a good model, which can show the way forward.[2]

To be sure, the excesses of the financial crisis originated in the financial centers of New York and London on the back of massive under-pricing of risk in housing markets and their obfuscation within complex financial products. Hence, referring to the

[1] Author's translation of, *Déclaration de M. Nicolas Sarkozy, Président de la République, sur la politique menée face à la crise économique et financière, à Toulon le 1er décembre 2009*. Available at: <http://discours.vie-publique.fr/ notices/097003488.html> [last accessed May 23, 2013].
[2] Angela Merkel speech to the World Economic Forum in Davos, Switzerland, January 30, 2009.

financial crisis in particular and reckless financial capitalism in general as *Anglo-Saxon* or *Anglo-American* seems reasonable and empirically valid. It is easy, then, to be tempted into thinking that significantly different models of capitalism exist in continental Europe. Yet, should such proclamations be accepted without skepticism? Do not the complex and vast interlinkages extant in the global economy in general and the world of finance in particular limit the degrees of difference among political economies, particularly those European political economies referred to by Sarkozy and Merkel?

The proclamations of political leaders such as the above find continued expression in parts of heterodox political economy, namely in the varieties of capitalism approach and similar variants, which we have discussed in Chapters 1–3. Recall that in terms of finance the varieties of capitalism approach holds that more organized forms of capitalism are characterized as bank-dominated, as opposed to market-dominated in the case of more liberal market economies (Culpepper 2005; Deeg 2009; Zysman 1983). Yet, in light of the financial crisis and significant failures of financial institutions within the so-called "coordinated market economies," and the revelation of complicity on the part of financial institutions from these political economies, it is important to reconsider whether the theorization of finance and financial systems within the varieties of capitalism approach is empirically sound. Indeed, some of the most notable bank failures at the beginning of the global financial crisis were German financial institutions that were highly exposed to risky subprime assets.[3] Like other countries

---

[3] One of the first casualties of the global financial crisis was Sachsen LB, the Landesbank of Free State of Saxony. In 2003 and 2004 the bank set up two special purpose investment conduits, Georges Quay and Ormond Quay respectively, through its wholly-owned subsidiary Sachsen LB Europe PLC located in Dublin, Ireland. These off balance sheet investment vehicles borrowed in the short-term commercial paper market and invested in longer-term structured credit instruments, the latter of which had significant exposure to U.S. subprime mortgages, which at the time were highly rated. At the end of 2003 the volume of funds in the conduits stood at circa €4 billion. By June 30, 2007, there was circa €26 billion invested. The Dublin operations easily became the most profitable business of Sachsen LB, with a return on equity exceeding 30 percent by 2005. Not

in Europe, the German government created a €480 billion rescue fund (roughly 13 percent of GDP), the *Sonderfonds Finanzmarktstabilisierung*, to bail out financial institutions affected by the crisis. Such major contagion suggests that the separation between and differentiation among political economies is not very significant.

If European financial institutions were so affected by the fallout of U.S. housing markets, it begs the question of whether an alternative European models exists, at least in the area of finance, or even if an alternative model can exist in the current global political–economic conjuncture. Even if the ongoing Eurozone crisis highlights ongoing differences among European economies, the parlous state of affairs and the patent interdependence discounts the perceived salience of institutional diversity between countries, particularly in terms of the role of financial markets and financial institutions. This complicates the modeling and empirical verification of capitalist variety at the national macro-institutional level. Consequently, there is a need for a reevaluation of how and whether finance can continue to complement other institutional spheres within countries and in country-specific ways in influencing firms and other actors.

Eliciting the discussion on institutions and institutional change in Chapter 3 and our discussion in Chapter 1 on financial system change, the next section, Functional Equivalence in Finance, contrasts the theorization of finance and financial systems as offered by the varieties of capitalism with an

---

surprisingly another fund was started, Sachsen Funding, in the spring of 2007 just as crisis tremors emerged. This run in high finance quickly came to an end, as the asset-backed securities market began to tumble in the spring of 2007. By August 2007 Sachsen LB's conduits were unable to cover their liabilities in the short-term paper market. A banking pool of other Landesbanken and the Sparkassen-Finanzgruppe, the German association of savings banks, provided €17.1 billion to the Ormond Quay conduit to cover its liabilities. As further investment losses eroded Sachen LB's equity capital to below regulatory standards, the bank's owner, the Free State of Saxony and the Sachsen Finanzgruppe (a state-owned holding company) had to find a suitable solution for the bank. On August 26, 2007 the owners concluded an agreement to sell Sachsen LB to Landesbank Baden-Württemburg (LBBW).

economic–geographical approach that is attentive to the functions of institutions, following the argument that institutional form is not necessarily determinate of institutional function. Empirical weight is added to the argument thereafter, first by considering changes to German corporate governance, and second, by comparing the changing functional and formal characteristics of the German financial system and banking sector with that of the United States since the beginning of the 1990s. These two countries are compared given that the former figures as the most ideal-typical coordinated market economy in the varieties of capitalism approach, while the latter figures as the most ideal-typical liberal market economy. Comparing these two countries is therefore an appropriate case selection for assessing theoretical applicability. It is shown that the financial systems of the two countries are increasingly similar in form; and where they continue to diverge in form, common functions produce analogous outcomes.

Functional Equivalence in Finance

Patient Capital

Recall that in the varieties of capitalism framework the primary difference in corporate finance between coordinated and liberal market economies is the presumed existence of "patient capital." The existence of patient capital in coordinated market economies allows firms to invest in projects that produce returns only in the long run and to retain a skilled workforce through economic downturns. Patient capital depends crucially on investors having access to inside information concerning the operation of the firm. As such, finance does not depend on balance sheet criteria, as is the case in a liberal market economy. The provision of information concerning the progress of firms in coordinated market economies occurs through dense networks that link managers and technical personnel of a firm to counterparts in other firms and industry associations. Information sharing also occurs through networks of cross-shareholding, where different firms are represented on the boards of other firms. Firm strategies in coordinated market economies also rely on tax provisions and securities regulations that limit the scope for hostile takeovers, thus reducing a firm's sensitivity to short-term profitability.

The existence of patient capital is presumed to be a function of the institutional form of the financial system. Mirroring the binary logic, coordinated market economies are characterized as bank-based systems, whereas liberal market economies are characterized as market-based systems wherein capital is hypothesized to be impatient. The criteria for determining this distinction are quantitative measures of the ratio of equity market capitalization to GDP and the level of household savings in marketable securities, the latter being largely a function of the form of the pension system.[4] A key characteristic of bank-based systems is that households place a large proportion of their savings in bank deposits.

The presumed formal difference between a bank-based system and a market-based system is that the former mediates the flow of savings and investment through close trust-based relationships between the lender and the borrower. In bank-based systems, banks are significant providers of loans to non-financial firms, in which they also typically participate in firms' governance and strategy through large equity holdings and board membership; as such, bank loans represent a large portion of corporate liabilities. Banks in bank-based systems, while also being important nodes in the nexus of corporate governance relations, also play an important role in influencing other parts

---

[4] Using market capitalization to GDP is not a very reliable comparative statistic, as market valuations represent investors' expectation on future cash flows. A country with a high market capitalization to GDP ratio could simply reflect perceptions that the economy's long-term prospects are good. Market capitalization to GDP does not provide sufficient information about how firms actually employ capital.

of the financial services sector, such as stock markets and investment firms. In a market-based financial system, on the contrary, capital mediation occurs through arm's length market transactions. In this context, it is assumed that firms are under pressure to maximize shareholder value in the short term.

The Pecking Order of Corporate Finance

An economic–geographical perspective of firm finance takes a different approach, questioning whether the form of the financial system determines how firms acquire external financing or whether firm financing is a function of variables specific to the firm. One way of interrogating this question is through the Pecking Order Theory, which contends that firm characteristics such as size, age, and growth potential are the primary drivers of how firms acquire, have access to, and employ capital (Myers 1984). Accordingly, firms prioritize their sources of financing consistent with the principle of least effort. As such, firms prefer internal financing in the first instance. If external financing is needed, firms will prefer debt first, followed by a hybrid security such as a convertible bond, and finally equity. As many small and medium-sized enterprises are frequently manager-owned or family-owned, there is often a preference for those forms of finance that limit outside intrusion in the business.

This theory manifests in the data. For instance, in a study using flow of funds data from national accounting statistics, Corbett and Jenkinson (1996, 1997) calculate the net sources and uses of funds over the period 1970–1994 for investment in physical assets by non-financial corporate firms in Germany, the United States, the United Kingdom, and Japan. This period is noteworthy, as the distinction between market-based versus bank-based financial systems was prevalent in academic debates. For the United States and the United Kingdom, internal sources financed 96.1 percent and 93.3 percent, respectively, of all physical investment. For Japan and Germany, internal sources financed 69.9 percent and 78.9 percent, respectively, of all physical investment. In all cases the majority of external financing came from banks. Bank financing represented 11.9 percent in Germany, 11.1 percent in the United States, 26.7 percent in Japan, and 14.6 percent in the United Kingdom, of all physical investment (see also Rajan and Zingales 1995). These findings concur with Edwards and Fischer's (1994) study that shows that bank loans did not finance a larger proportion of investment by non-financial firms in Germany during the 1970s and 1980s in comparison to the United Kingdom, a purportedly market-based system.

But the preference of internal finance over external finance is not simply a function of choice. Smaller firms in particular are in general informationally opaque, and lenders cannot be assured that credit will be employed in a productive manner. As a result, credit providers may charge a higher risk premium or demand collateral often greater than available firm assets such that obtaining external finance may be prohibitively expensive or impossible. The size and age of a firm affect this relationship, as larger and older firms normally possess a known track record and may have more assets to pledge as collateral. The sector in which the firm locates may also contribute to financing constraints, depending on the sector's economic prospects.

In general, it is only large corporations or firms with a high growth potential that are able to issue traded securities (e.g. stocks, bonds, commercial paper). In terms of equity, the costs of going public are considerable, and young and small firms may have to accept a significant discount on their fair value from investors due to an insufficient track record. Moreover, companies that go public lose confidentiality and complete control (Pagano et al. 1998). Private equity and venture capital likewise is not available to most firms. Financiers in this area of intermediation look to invest in firms that can be acquired at a significant discount or possess significant growth potential. In effect, most firms, notwithstanding the categorization of the financial system, rely almost exclusively on banks for their external financing needs (Beck et al. 2008).

Cumulative Patient Capital

In the second instance, it is important to question whether the relationship between form and function in finance is this direct and asymmetric. Recall the argument in Chapter 1 that financial functions are more stable than the institutional form of the financial system. In historical perspective, financial functions have varied less across geopolitical borders and have changed less over time than institutional form. Accordingly, institutional form and the corporate identity of financial intermediaries may vary across countries for a number of reasons, such as size, complexity, available technology, and political and cultural traditions, yet the basic economic functions remain the same: to facilitate the allocation and deployment of economic resources across time and space.

If the functions of a financial system vary less than the institutional form, it follows that different types of institutions—including those acting in the space of the market—can provide equivalent functions in a financial system. Consequently, it cannot be assumed that banks, as opposed to other institutions, are more apt to provide "patient capital". This complicates the logic in the varieties of capitalism approach that the institutional form of one system functionally provides more patient capital as opposed to another system with a different institutional form. Markets are generally made up of short-term, medium-term, and long-term players (Bushee 2004).[5] For example, just like a bank,

---

[5] Bushee (2004) classifies institutional investors in three categories: (1) transient institutions, which exhibit high portfolio turnover and own small stakes in portfolio companies; (2) dedicated institutions, which provide stable ownership and take large positions in individual firms; (3) quasi-indexers, which trade infrequently and hold small stakes in firms. Analyzing U.S. institutional investors during the period 1983–2002, Bushee found that 31 percent were transient institutions, 8 percent were dedicated institutions, and 61 percent were quasi-indexers. This suggests that a majority of institutional investors are oriented to medium and long-term time horizons.

large institutional investors have the capacity to acquire information, monitor managers, and exert corporate control. The institutional function of many large investors, such as pension funds and mutual funds, is to ensure stable long-term financial performance that exceeds and/or matches the performance of the market. In so doing, such institutional investors must balance long-term objectives with short-term exigencies of the market under conditions of risk and uncertainty. These exigencies may demand at times a high turnover of assets, as failure to do so may impair their long-term objectives. Nonetheless, the combination of long-term objectives coupled with the status of large institutional investors as "universal owners" such that collectively they own a large proportion of publicly traded securities and that their cumulative long-term return is determined not by the performance of a single firm but by the performance of the economy, suggests that they function in aggregate as providers of patient capital to capital users (Hawley and Williams 2000, 2007).

Consider this example further. Even though the market for corporate bonds is presumed to function as an arm's length transaction between the firm and investor, a bond market can functionally mimic bank lending. In obtaining a loan from a bank a firm submits to monitoring and control by the bank, which may come at a cost and distort a firm's incentives (Rajan 1992). Yet this has to be weighed against the benefits of the informationally intense relationship, which can facilitate continued lending over time. This is particularly apposite for more opaque firms. Larger more transparent firms, on the other hand, may prefer to avoid the potential costs associated with bank lending by issuing debt at arm's length to investors in the bond market. However, when the firm wants to issue new debt securities it utilizes an investment bank (usually in syndicate with other banks) to place the debt in the market. There is nothing in the formal structure of the market that prevents the firm from utilizing the same lead investment bank every time it needs to issue new debt, particularly if the same bank engages in concurrent lending to the firm (Drucker and Puri 2005). As an intermediary, the investment bank can utilize and act as a delegated monitor in continually acquiring information about the firm for a stable set of institutional investors that purchase the debt.

One need not look, however, at the existence of long-term agents in the market to consider the existence of a long-term focus. As Roe (2012) has pointed out, markets can actually be overly long-term in focus. Take, for example, the dot-com bubble at the beginning of the millennium where an entire sector became hugely overvalued. While such high valuations pointed to a bubble, it also suggested a market looking forward toward the future. Although many firms failed and had no hope of ever achieving a level of revenue and profit necessary to justify their high valuation, some survived and new ones continue to arrive on the scene. Many of the large technology firms now, such as Apple or Amazon, continue to have relatively high market capitalizations. This ultimately reflects the market's appreciation of the long-term earnings potential of these firms. Where the market appears to be oriented to the short term, this may not have anything to do with actions of financial agents within and without the firm driving a short-term orientation. Rather, it likely reflects a rapidly changing technological environment or the continued emergence of new competitors at home and abroad. As both cases suggest, qualifying the market as necessarily a short-term institution limits its actual functional scope.

Restructuring Tradition

Beginning in the early 1990s important systemic reforms have driven financial market development, ultimately expanding the range of financing options for non-financial firms. Part of this development has coincided with Germany's attempt, like other advanced and emerging economies, to capture an increasing share of global GDP related to financial services, which London and New York have long cornered (Faulconbridge

2004). Accordingly, reforms were initiated to raise the status of Frankfurt, and thus German financial services providers, as a global financial center under the name of *Finanzplatz Deutschland* (Story and Walter 1997). As the major financial centers operated on market logics with vast product offerings and different forms of financing, coupled with important investor protections, German regulation would begin to move in that direction.[6]

Promoting Markets

A key functional imperative of investors in global financial markets is transparency and the protection of minority shareholder rights, or rather, the interests of outsiders. The reasons for protecting minority shareholder rights are twofold. First, limited protection of minority shareholders restricts the ability to attract foreign firms to list their equity on the domestic stock exchange. Foreign firms are more likely to list in markets that are

---

[6] Another factor of financial transformation has been the reform of the German pension system. Beginning with reforms in 1992 and subsequent reforms in 1997 and 2001, the relative generosity—the income replacement rate of final salary—of the pay-as-you-go public system was progressively reduced, necessitating the increase of private funded pension arrangements. Private occupational pensions existed for some workers in large firms, but these were largely in the form of book reserves on corporate balance sheets. Yet also during this period, many large firms began to transfer book reserves into funded pension trusts, turning them effectively into Anglo-American styled pension funds. The 2001 "Riester" Reform, named after the then labor minister Walter Riester, introduced new occupational and personal pension plans, whose uptake the government supported with tax concessions. As a result, whereas the existence of pension fund capital was previously limited, these reforms set the stage for significant asset accumulation and support for the German financial services industry (Burger 2012; Dixon 2009). Over the last few decades, the portfolio composition of German households has changed as a consequence. In 1980, 60 percent of household financial wealth was held in currency and bank deposits. By 2000, this had dropped to roughly 40 percent. During that time households acquired more equities, either through direct holdings or mutual funds, from a base of just below 5 percent. Yet, this upward trend peaked at roughly 25 percent at the height of the dot-com stock market boom in the late 1990s. Since then, German households have been reluctant to wade into stock market investing. Hence, equity holdings have declined to just below 20 percent of household portfolios. In contrast, holdings of insurance and pension products has increased steadily from slightly above 20 percent to over 35 percent of household financial holdings (see De Bonis et al. 2013).

deeply liquid. Increasing liquidity, however, requires increasing the pool of potential investors, both domestic and foreign. Yet without sufficient transparency and the protection of minority rights, investors are less likely to invest in such markets. Second, in the process of protecting minority shareholder rights, the potential investor pool for domestic firms increases as it becomes necessary to ensure that the domestic market provides sufficient liquidity and opportunity for domestic firms, which face fewer constraints in listing and raising capital in foreign markets. In other words, limiting defection of domestic firms to foreign markets requires providing similar conditions extant in other more liquid markets, such as New York and London.

Four significant legislative reforms were passed beginning in 1990 for the promotion of financial markets: the *Erstes* (1990), *Zweites* (1994), *Drittes* (1998), and *Viertes* (2002) *Finanzmarktförderungsgesetzt*. The second of these legislative agendas was the most significant. Effectively, the Second Law created the *Bundesanstalt für Finanzdienstleistungsaufsicht* (Federal Securities Trading Commission), which was set up to enforce U.S.-style securities market traditions of protecting minority shareholder rights and transparency in trading (Vitols 2005). These changes were not simply driven at the local level. As mentioned in Chapter 1, European legislation, in conjunction with the Financial Services Action Plan of 1999 and the Single European Act of 1986, has been a key driver behind the creation of a single market for financial services along the lines of a more market-based system.

In addition to securities market regulations, financial transformation has been driven through corporate governance reform, beginning with the 1998 company law reform the *Gesetz zur Kontrolle und Transparenz im Unternehmensbereich* (KonTraG). This legislation extended the liability of supervisory and management boards, as well as that of accountants, as a means of increasing corporate transparency and ultimately to protect the interests of outside investors. The legislation also abolished unequal voting rights, placed limits on proxy voting by banks, and allowed firms to provide compensation through stock options and to conduct share buy-backs (Cioffi 2002). In effect, public firms were allowed (or coerced) to follow practices similar to those available in Anglo-American jurisdictions. This has led to increasing convergence in corporate governance standards across Europe, particularly in the area of disclosure (Bauer et al. 2008; O'Sullivan 2000; Wójcik 2006).

The Great Unraveling

The major shift of corporate governance in practice manifested itself in the large private universal banks' (Deutsche Bank, Commerzbank and Dresdner Bank) divesting their equity stakes in large German firms (Beyer 2003). Up to the 1990s the large private universal banks were the primary lenders to, and played extensive roles in the governance of, large German firms, holding blocks of shares and seats on corporate boards across industries. As significant owners of corporate equity—a legal impossibility in the United States—the large universal banks also dominated stock markets, thus shaping any potential hostile struggles for corporate control (Roe 2003). It was this close relationship between large banks and large firms that underpinned much of the conceptual apparatus of bank-based corporate governance and finance in comparative institutionalist research.

Whereas hostile takeovers had previously been legally and institutionally difficult, the hostile takeover of Mannsemann AG by Vodafone plc of the United Kingdom in 1999/2000 for more than €150 billion marked the end of an era, bringing the market for corporate control that swept U.S. and U.K. markets in the 1980s and 1990s home to Germany (Höpner and Jackson 2006). Indeed, the postwar period was characterized by a paucity of hostile takeovers, given high ownership concentration. Banks' equity ownership was not actually that significant in comparison to other large shareholders, yet banks were influential through the exercise of proxy voting rights and because of voting restrictions. The proportion of shares of large German firms that were widely held was often held with banks, to which the banks were granted voting rights (Franks and Mayer 2001). Although a voluntary takeover code existed from 1995, a more formal takeover law, *Gesetz zur Regelung von offentlichen Angeboten zum Erwerb von Wertpapieren und von Unternehmensubernahmen*, was introduced in 2002. This law is modeled after the London City Code, though with some modifications, which gave supervisory boards some power to defend against hostile bids (Kirchner and Painter 2002).

As the large private banks divested their shares, many large German firms started to dilute local ownership concentration in favor of more dispersed national and international ownership comparable to their corporate counterparts in Anglo-American markets. This coincided with Anglo-American institutional investors entering the German market in greater numbers, as part of global portfolio diversification strategies. Accordingly, the insulated world of German corporate governance and finance has started to look increasingly Anglo-American in scope and practice (Wójcik 2002). The entrance of large portfolio investors was important as it offered large firms new sources of financing, while also making them more prone to market pricing and thus market discipline. Bankers are still represented on the boards of non-financial firms, but their numbers are roughly in line with the representation of bankers on the boards of U.S. non-financial firms. There is limited evidence to suggest that bankers strongly monitor management, which in theory is supposed to distinguish bank-based systems from market-based systems. Some suggest that their representation on German corporate boards is used, rather, to promote their services as lenders and mergers and acquisitions advisors (Dittmann et al. 2010).

Yet, even if large firms are adjusting to the global mean demanded of the market, most firms in Germany are excluded from public securities markets and many of these larger institutional transformations affect them mostly indirectly. However, this is not unique to Germany. In the United States there are around 21,410 public companies, yet roughly 7.7 million employer firms. SMEs, classified as employing 500 persons or less, represent 80 percent of private sector employment. Most of these are privately held. In Germany there are roughly 1,498 public companies, and roughly 3.5 million SMEs, representing 70.5 percent of private sector employment.[7] If so many firms are excluded from market-based forms of external finance, then drawing macro-institutional hypotheses about the behavior of economic agents based on a binary logic of bank-based versus market-based financial system may not provide satisfactory conclusions on aggregate firm behavior. This does not imply that macro-institutional distinctions for the vast majority of firms that depend on bank-based finance cannot be made. Yet, as the following section, Banking in Germany and the United States, shows, making such distinctions would be difficult, as macro-institutional differences between the respective banking systems of Germany and the United States have become less salient.

Banking in Germany and the United States

Despite the label of a market-based financial system, banks form a major part of financial intermediation in the U.S. financial system. While the ratio of bank assets to GDP in Germany significantly exceeds that of the United States, as illustrated in Table 4.1 for the period 1999–2008, the ratio of bank assets to GDP has grown much faster in the United States than in Germany, as has GDP. That total asset growth in the United States grew nearly 100 percent over the period highlights the significance

---

[7] The data described here come from several sources from different time periods, but within a five-year period. Data on number of establishments and employees are for 2008. See 2012 U.S. Census Bureau Statistical Abstract Table 758; Institut für Mittelstandsforschung Bonn "Schlüsselzahlen des Mittelstands in Deutschland 2007/2008", available at <http://www.ifm-bonn.org>. Data on the number of public companies for the United States and Germany are for early 2013 and are sourced from Credit Risk Monitor, available at <http://www.crmz.com> [last accessed June 14, 2013].

Table 4.1 Bank assets to GDP

Year	Germany		United States	
	1999	2008	1999	2008
Bank assets[a]	4767323	6585121	7178077	14286520
GDP[a]	2012000	2495800	9301000	14369400
Percent	237	264	77	99
Growth over period				
Bank assets		38%		99%
GDP		24%		54%

[a]*Current prices in millions of national currency.*

Source: OECD Bank Profitability Statistics.

of bank-based financial intermediation. The large difference in the ratio of bank assets to GDP is partly accounted for by differences in institutional coverage in the statistical reporting. Here, only U.S. banking operations covered by deposit insurance, and regulated as such, are accounted for. In effect, a large range of non-depository financial intermediaries is excluded, which fulfills comparable banking functions. In contrast, the existence of universal banking in Germany contributes to broader institutional coverage of financial intermediation in the economy. An alternative means of comparing banking in the two countries is by looking at the number of banking establishments.

As illustrated in Table 4.2, the United States has an extensive banking establishment as compared with Germany. Again, these data only account for U.S. banking establishments covered by deposit insurance regimes. The United States, with an economy roughly four times as large as the German economy, possesses a large cooperative sector and exceeds Germany in the number of commercial banks. The two banking markets share similarities in that most banking establishments have a regional remit, which is partly attributable to their respective federal political systems (Maalouf 2006).

Where the two markets diverge in institutional form is that the United States does not have public banks. However, as the next two subsections (The Evolution of German Banking, and

Table 4.2 Banks and bank branches in 2010

	Germany		United States	
	Number	Branches	Number	Branches
Public sector banks	10	471	n/a	n/a
Landesbanken				
Sparkassen	429	13,025	n/a	n/a
Cooperative banks				
Cooperatives (central institutions)	2	11	n/a	n/a
Cooperatives	1,141	12,046	7,339[a]	—
Membership (in millions)	*17*		*90.5*	
Percent of total population	*21*		*29*	
Commercial banks	300	10,826	6,529[b]	82,641
Savings banks (private)	13	976	1,128[b]	—

[a]*NCUA Insured.*

[b]*FDIC Insured.*

Source: Deutsche Bundesbank; Federal Deposit Insurance Corporation (FDIC); National Credit Union Association (NCUA).

Banking in America) demonstrate, the formal difference between public and private in the German case has become increasingly marginal, as public guarantees covering the banks' lending activities have been phased out. And although the United States lacks a public bank sector with explicit functional mandates to foster local economic development, a variety of functionally equivalent mechanisms exist to counter market failure and encourage local economic development.

The Evolution of German Banking

The German banking system has been classified as a three-pillar system (Brunner et al. 2004; Hackethal 2004). The first pillar consists of the large private banks, which includes Deutsche Bank, Commerzbank, Deutsche Postbank, and HypoVereinsbank, as well as smaller commercial banks. The second pillar consists of the public sector banks: the regional savings banks (Sparkassen) and the Landesbanken. The third pillar consists of the cooperative sector, which consists of smaller cooperative banks and

Table 4.3 Market share in 2009 by category of bank

	Commercial banks	Public sector[a]	Cooperatives[b]	Special purpose banks	Mortgage banks and building associations
Loans to banks	0.30	0.32	0.12	0.16	0.11
Loans to non-banks	0.27	0.36	0.13	0.08	0.16
Loans to domestic enterprises and self-employed enterprises	0.26	0.41	0.11	0.13	0.08
Manufacturing sector	*0.35*	*0.41*	*0.03*	*0.13*	*0.08*
Housing loans	0.24	0.33	0.19	0.05	0.19

[a]Landesbanken and Sparkassen.
[b]Including cooperative central banks.

Source: Deutsche Bundesbank Banking Statistics.

two cooperative central banks, DZ Bank and WGZ Bank. An additional pillar exists in the form of specialist banks, such as state-owned development bank KfW, SME lender IKB Deutsche Industriebank, and mortgage banks.

Despite the formal classification of the three pillars, functional differences among the three are limited. Banks in Germany are universal banks, meaning that they can offer a broad range of financial services to their clients, such as deposit taking, consumer and commercial lending, securities underwriting and trading, investment management, and insurance and pension services (Grunson and Schneider 1995). In effect, the three main pillars compete across the spectrum of financial intermediation. So, like the large private banks, the Landesbanken and the two cooperative central banks are actively engaged in providing a wide range of lending and capital market services, such as derivatives trading and structured finance. While market shares of different intermediation activities vary, no domain is exclusive to one pillar. This is particularly true in the loan market, illustrated in Table 4.3, where no single pillar holds a majority of the market across major loan segments. Moreover, the three pillars all have active operations outside of Germany.

The private sector, particularly Deutsche Bank, does lead in capital market operations. Yet, even in this segment the Landesbanken and the cooperative central banks are active. For instance, in 2009 DZ Bank and Landesbank Baden-Württemberg ranked 22 and 23 with market shares of 0.9 percent each in Thomson Financial's book runner league table for European corporate bond issues. This compares to Commerzbank's 13th place ranking with a market share of 2.4 percent and Deutsche Bank's 1st place ranking with a market share of 10.4 percent.

Historically, the defining institutional form between the pillars has been the public law status of the Landesbanken and their ownership by their respective Länder. With this institutional form came a functional mandate to develop local economic capacity, in order to counter market failure, for which they received statutory liability guarantees. This public mandate meant, in theory, that development of the regional economy should supersede any profit maximizing objectives. Yet in practice, Landesbanken have not been *stricto sensu* institutions solely in pursuit of regional economic prosperity (Sinn 1999). Moreover, the Landesbanken have been criticized for being structurally unprofitable and prone to risk-taking (Hau and Thum 2009). Landesbanken have long provided services to domestic and international customers, governments, corporations, and individuals and their activities have not remained confined to the home region. Branches of Landesbanken have existed for several decades in major international financial centers such as New York and London (Grunson and Schneider 1995).

In the late-1990s European private banks began to challenge the system of state guarantees provided to Landesbanken by regional governments, known as *Anstaltslast* (deficiency guarantee) and *Gewährträgerhaftung* (maintenance guarantee), arguing that the guarantees provided for favorable long-term credit ratings for the public institutions. The private bank sector argued that this put them at a competitive disadvantage vis-à-vis the Landesbanken, which were competing in the same markets and operating beyond the original intent of their regional mandates, thus contravening European competition law in respect of state aid. While the issue of privatization had surfaced from time to time, particularly as privatization of government-owned enterprises became popular across affluent democracies in the last few decades of the twentieth century, the principles of competition set forth by European Union legislation brought the issue to the fore (Grossman 2006; Lütz 2004).

In December 1999 the European Banking Federation filed a complaint with the Directorate General of Competition of the European Commission. Following an inquiry, the Commission and the German authorities reached an agreement in July 2001 to abolish *Gewährträgerhaftung* and to curtail *Anstaltslast*; liabilities made until that point would be grandfathered in and guaranteed until July 2005, after which the guarantees would cease. In effect, by the middle of 2005 the protective umbrella of state guarantees would no longer cover the Landesbanken, leveling the playing field among financial institutions and further eroding the formal distinctiveness of different categories of banks in Germany.

Such distinctiveness has been further eroded as several public sector banks, specifically HSH Nordbank AG (which resulted from the merger between Hamburg LB and LB Schleswig-Holstein), LandesBank Berlin AG, and the now defunct WestLB AG (North Rhine-Westphalia), were converted into joint stock companies (Aktiengesellschaft) operating under private law. Ownership in the cases of LandesBank Berlin and West LB remained with Länder governments and other public entities. Yet, in the case of HSH Nordbank the change in legal status involved new private capital.[8] Whereas some Landesbanken were privatized, other Länder governments simply revised legislation removing the guarantees, while maintaining the public law status of the Landesbank. The only guarantee that exists now is the implicit

---

[8] In 2006 US-based private equity firm J.C. Flowers established nine trusts to acquire 26.6 percent ownership of HSH Nordbank. This share has since been diluted to less than 10 percent following recapitalization of the bank by the German government in 2008 in the face of significant subprime-related losses.

guarantee that could potentially come with public ownership. If formal differences do matter, then they should matter most in terms of reducing financing constraints for firms. However, it has been shown that public ownership of banks is not correlated with a reduction in financing constraints for firms (Engel and Middendorf 2009). Ultimately, whether a distinction between public and private banks continues to exist is uncertain.

Where a functional distinction might be assumed to exist in the difference between private and public, including the cooperative sector, is in the strategic focus of the Sparkassen and the smaller cooperative banks. While all three pillars lend to the SME sector, the Sparkassen and cooperative banks show a greater propensity to lend to small and young firms, particularly outside major urban areas, whereas the larger private banks have tended to focus on larger SMEs (Prantl et al. 2009). Given their size, the Sparkassen and cooperative banks are considered to be relationship lenders, where credit provision is based on inside information obtained by the bank through a long-term relationship with the firm.

Yet this institutional environment had undergone important changes over the last decade in the run-up to the introduction of the Basel II Capital Accords in 2007. Basel II introduced joint minimum equity standards and unified criteria for measuring lending risks, requiring all banks to link SME lending to detailed information and formalized credit-rating procedures. As such, bank relationships have become more sensitive to firm profitability and future prospects (Bluhm and Martens 2009). These new procedures further the scope and rationale for increased use of transactions-based lending technologies, which can occur at arm's length and for which larger banks maintain a comparative advantage due to economies of scale (Berger and Udell 2006).

While transactions-based lending may be on the increase, this does not mean that strong firm–bank relationships are diminishing. For instance, a study of 16,000 SMEs shows that 54.2 percent of firms in their sample raise at least 80 percent of their loans from one bank; 41 percent of firms have only one banking relationship, 22.2 percent have 2, and 12.1 percent have 3. In all, 90 percent of the firms have six relationships or fewer (Memmel et al. 2008). A low number of lending banks is considered to be an indicator of a close firm–bank relationship and/or the existence of a main bank, the so-called *hausbank* (Elsas 2005; Harhoff and Körting 1998). Nevertheless, such strong firm–bank relationships are not unique to the German case.

Banking in America

Like Germany, the U.S. banking sector is characterized as having a small number of very large banks and a large number of smaller banks, and a large cooperative sector. The coexistence of federal and state chartering, in existence since the end of the Civil War, fostered and reinforced the establishment of small institutions and fragmentation along state lines. This was furthered by various state and federal regulations, such as the McFadden Act of 1927, which prohibited interstate branch banking. There was a fear of concentration, which was reflected in both state and federal regulations (Critchfield et al. 2004). As a result, the number of small banks flourished across the country. By 1980 there were 14,434 chartered commercial banks, 97 percent of which had less than $1 billion (2001 dollars) in assets (DeYoung 2007). Fragmentation along state lines thus focused the remit of most banks on economic development at state level. Intrastate regulation on geographic location further focused the activities of banks on local economic development. While the institutional form of this function relies on private agents in comparison to the German case where public agents were relied on in addition to private agents, the institutional functions between the two institutional forms is comparable.

In the 1970s, financial innovation and technological change began to reorder the traditional bank delivery system in the United States. For instance, money market mutual funds provided households and small businesses an alternative to traditional bank deposits for their liquid assets. Credit cards also began to appear, which were offered by larger national banks. In the 1980s, regulatory changes began to reduce further the strict bordering of banking activity that innovation and technological change were already leading. Interstate banking began to grow slowly, as states entered into reciprocity agreements, taking advantage of the multibank holding company loophole in the McFadden Act. However, the zenith of banking deregulation came in the 1990s. In 1994 the United States Congress passed the Riegle-Neal Interstate Banking and Branching Efficiency Act, which repealed restrictions on interstate banking. This resulted in a massive wave of bank merger activity, which saw mega-mergers between large commercial banks and consolidation in the community bank sector (DeYoung et al. 2004). In 1999 the United States Congress passed the Graham-Leach-Bliley Act, which repealed the Glass-Steagall Act separating commercial and investment banks. This allowed for universal banking as existed already in European banking markets. Consequently, differences in institutional form between Germany and the United States, at least for very large banking institutions, became even more similar.

Despite deregulation, many of the geographic features of the pre-deregulation period have remained. While the number of small community banks slightly more than halved, the numbers have stabilized and those that remain are shown to be competitive in terms of profitability and market share vis-à-vis larger banks (Berger et al. 2007; Jones and Critchfield 2005). In effect, the vast majority of banking establishments still have a limited geographic reach such that the geography of banking in the United States is still decentralized, much like the German case. In effect, the institutional basis for the provision of credit at the local level remains intact. Only the very large banks have a national presence, and even among large mid-sized banks (with assets of more than $1 billion, but smaller than the largest 25 banks) many are focused on particular regions of the country (Gratton 2004).

A more surprising trend has been the significant growth in bank branches. Between 1990 and 2008, the total number of commercial bank branches, not including savings institutions and credit unions, grew from 50,858 to 90,018.[9] Banking strategies have bifurcated by size class, with larger banks leveraging their scale advantages in offering high volume, low value-added transactions banking products, whereas smaller banks focus more on low volume, high value-added relationship banking (Berger and Udell 2002; Elyasiani and Goldberg 2004; Udell 2008). This suggests that strong firm–bank relationships, comparable to the German case, remain an important component of financial intermediation in the United States (Cole et al. 2004). The small number of lending relationships that firms maintain substantiates this inference. In the last Survey of Small Business Finances conducted by the Federal Reserve and the Small Business Administration in 2003, a nationally representative cross-sectional survey of SMEs, the average number of commercial banks from which a firm obtained financial services was 1.246 (Cole 2008). Ultimately, such bifurcation between large and small U.S. banks is comparable to the German case discussed above, where the Sparkassen and cooperatives focus on small-scale local operations and larger banks maintain larger operations at a broader geographical scale.

While the continued decentralization of the U.S. banking system provides a structural form conducive to local and regional development, it is worth noting that federal law has reinforced the functional agency of banks in providing for local and regional development needs. This is particularly evident in the Community Reinvestment Act (CRA). Passed by the United States Congress in 1977 the CRA stipulates that "regulated financial institutions have continuing and affirmative obligation to help meet the credit needs of the local communities in which they are chartered."[10] The CRA, which applies to Federal Deposit Insurance Corporation (FDIC) covered institutions, was formulated in response to redlining practices and the refusal of banks to lend sufficiently in minority and low- and moderate-income

---

[9] See U.S. Census Bureau 2010 Statistical Abstract Table 1140.
[10] 12 U.S.C. §§ 2901–2907 (2013).

communities nationwide. The CRA works by requiring federal agencies to review periodically and report publicly whether a bank is fulfilling community credit needs. If found that a bank is not performing sufficiently in this regard, then a bank's plan to expand its operations could be denied. The CRA gives voice to local community groups in this process (Marsico 2004; Taylor and Silver 2008). As a result, it has been shown to positively influence the supply of credit in low- and middle-income communities (Barr 2005; Immergluck 2004; Kobeissi 2009).

In addition to such functional mandates as the CRA, the federal government is a major underwriter of small business loans channeled through private sector banks. The Small Business Administration (SBA) oversees a variety of loan guarantee programs that are aimed at improving the private market's allocation of credit to small business. This has been correlated with improved employment conditions in low-income markets (Craig et al. 2008). In fiscal year 2010 the SBA guaranteed 54,833 business loans; the SBA's total loan portfolio was worth $93.34 billion.[11] Ultimately, the U.S. banking system may not possess a distinguishable public sector banking pillar as exists in Germany, yet a variety of coordinating mechanisms exist to mitigate market failure and encourage local development. Indeed, the U.S. federal government has a long history of enhancing credit flows in private financial markets through government-sponsored enterprises (e.g. Fannie Mae, Freddie Mac, and Farmer Mac).

Conclusions

As the analysis demonstrates, the German financial system has converged closer in form and function to that of the United States. German, and in turn pan-European, financial regulation increasingly adheres to the tenets of transparency and the

[11] See *Summary of Performance and Financial Information Fiscal Year 2010*, U.S. Small Business Administration, Washington, DC.

protection of minority investors. As a result, large German firms increasingly face similar imperatives demanded of global financial markets that confront large public firms elsewhere. This has made it difficult to categorize the institutional form of the German financial system as bank-based. Yet, for most German firms external finance is still obtained from banks. However, this is equally the case in the United States and other capitalist economies, which complicates the use of the bank-based versus market-based binary as an explanatory device for understanding aggregate firm behavior. In comparing banking in Germany and the United States, it was shown that both countries have strong institutional similarities in function and increasingly in form. Both countries possess a mix of small and large banks, primarily distributed along regional lines. In both cases the market structure and geographical distribution provides the formal institutional scope for strong firm–bank relationships and the potential for patient capital, which is evidenced by the low degree of firm–bank relationships.

The significance of the observed convergence and the manifest functional and formal similarity between these two cases is that they demonstrate the challenge of determining the boundaries and therefore the causal significance of national (and local) institutions in shaping the behavior of economic agents in a world replete with cross-border flows of people, capital, and ideas. Indeed, ongoing economic globalization buttressed by capitalist market imperatives that are global in scope is creating a new macro-institutional environment, challenging previously identifiable national capitalisms. Capitalism in the singular, not varieties of capitalism, increasingly defines the "rules of the game."

Nonetheless, as both cases showed, political economies have ways of coping with capitalist market imperatives and limiting market failures albeit at times with different institutional forms. Different institutional forms can and do perform similar functions (Rodríguez-Pose and Storper 2006). Recall, for example, that the public banks in Germany historically had a mandate to foster local economic development, whereas in the United States strict federal and state banking regulation focused the actions of private agents, which has been further reinforced by other public policies. So, while the analysis in this chapter does not shy away from asserting that convergence has taken place and that much similarity is evident, it does not make the claim that the two countries are converging to some unique political–economic form, nor does it deny the critical importance of national-level public policy and institutions in shaping the location of economic activity and the behavior of economic agents.

Greater attention to national-level political–economic differentiation in comparative political economy and economic geography is, in effect, still relevant. The challenge, however, is in showing how it is still relevant. Reading off broad categorical and patently asymmetric models of capitalism is a questionable strategy, particularly if such models problematically obfuscate significant formal and functional convergence, the existence of transnational interdependent economic relations, and significant regional and urban/rural differences within countries. For example, such asymmetric models may also undervalue socioeconomic conditions that deserve more critical interrogation, such as two-tiered labor markets, which have become more pronounced in continental Europe (Doellgast and Greer 2007). By digging down to institutional function to see whether institutions that appear different in form are somehow similar in a deeper underlying way, a baseline is established allowing for a more accurate determination of the variables that matter most in producing some outcome or another in some places versus others, within countries and across countries. This strategy is apposite, moreover, if such variables are difficult to capture informal institutions. By this logic, it becomes possible to observe and define structural contingency at different scales with greater confidence.

5

Financialization and the Welfare State

The global population is aging. People are living longer and having fewer children. The median age in 2010 of the global population was 29. By 2050 it is projected to be 38, after which the pace of demographic aging is expected to slow. By 2100 it will be 42. For more developed parts of the world, aging has taken hold already, with the median age already having surpassed 40. But such significant demographic aging is not simply a rich-world phenomenon. While parts of sub-Saharan Africa are aging slowly in comparison, fast developing countries in East Asia are also aging quickly. The obvious consequence of demographic aging is an increase in the proportion of non-working individuals dependent on the working population. As Figure 5.1 shows, the current old-age dependency ratios for developed and less-developed regions are roughly 25 percent and 10 percent respectively; by 2050 these ratios will increase respectively to 45 percent and 23 percent.[1]

The macroeconomic implications of demographic aging are significant. As a country's population ages and more individuals

[1] The old-age dependency ratio is the ratio of the population aged 65 years or over to the population aged 15–64. More developed regions comprise Europe, North America, Australia/New Zealand, and Japan. Less developed regions comprise all regions of Africa, Asia (excluding Japan), Latin America and the Caribbean plus Melanesia, Micronesia, and Polynesia. The projections here show the medium fertility variant of the UN projections.

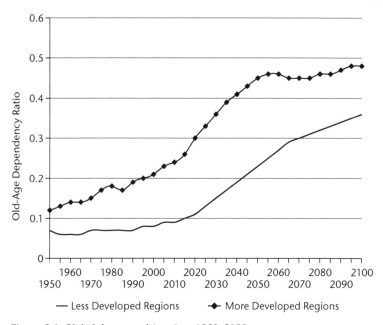

Figure 5.1 Global demographic aging, 1950–2100

Source: Population Division of the Department of Economic and Social Affairs of the United Nations Secretariat, World Population Prospects: The 2010 Revision.

enter retirement, the ratio of labor to total population decreases. If this decrease is not substituted with increases in productivity or increases in the capital stock, then total output decreases. Lower economic output means lower tax receipts and lower social security contributions, and thus more strain on the viability of public pay-as-you-go retirement systems, publicly funded healthcare, and other government expenditures such as education and infrastructure (Barr 2001). Increasing taxes, redistributing wealth, or increasing government debt to finance increasing social security obligations only provide a short- to medium-term solution to this longer-term problem—if such strategies are at all possible politically. Moreover, forgoing other expenditure, such as education spending or spending on research and development for social security financing, may lower long-term growth prospects for the economy, thus reinforcing the long-term fiscal predicament. At issue is how the active labor force will be able to provide adequate social security coverage in the form of retirement-income support and healthcare provision to an increasing proportion of the population without placing major strains on the economy. The implications for social cohesion and intergenerational equity can be profound (Auerbach et al. 1999).

If fiscal relief is more easily found in reforming public pensions rather than healthcare, the answer for most countries has come down to shifting part of the burden away from public pay-as-you-go pension schemes to private pre-funded arrangements reliant on the performance of financial markets. However, as empirical tests have shown, this has not meant necessarily that provision converges on a singular mode across countries, or that there is a race to the bottom in terms of retrenchment (see e.g. Castles 2004; Obinger et al. 2010; Swank 2002). The institutional setting, interest-group politics, and maturity of the public pension system act to limit the degree of convergence (at least in the short to medium term) (Immergut et al. 2007; Myles and Pierson 2001).

Even when the structure of public pension systems has remained stable albeit in the wake of increasing individualization and privatization, many governments across the globe have begun in recent years to partially pre-fund public pension obligations, recognizing that implicit pension debt represents a possible inter-temporal fiscal constraint. Governments have recognized that financial markets may penalize them in sovereign debt markets if this implicit pension debt is not effectively managed (Palacios 2003). Significantly, the pre-funding of future pension obligations has gone well beyond creating government trust funds laden with a country's own sovereign debt, as is the case in the United States and Spain for example. Many of these new pension reserve funds have adopted portfolio investment strategies comparable to other large and sophisticated pension funds, diversifying into international equities and real assets (e.g. infrastructure and real estate). These state-sponsored pension reserve funds and other sovereign wealth funds are becoming important global institutional investors in their own right (Clark et al. 2013).

Again, what is crucial, regardless of the degree to which pre-funding enters the retirement-income paradigm of a particular social security system, is that retirement income has become increasingly dependent on capital returns, and thus the prospects of financial markets that are increasingly global in scope. Notwithstanding the neoliberal political ideology often associated with or attributed to public pension restructuring (for such critiques, see Blackburn 2002, 2006; Minns 2001; see also Orenstein 2008), the shift to capitalized pension arrangements of all types, including the creation of pension reserve funds, is fundamentally about capturing global growth and diversifying the asset base on which social security is financed beyond the national economy. The geography of production has changed and with that the ability of national economies to capture and contain the value generated from economic growth and development, through the loss of the power (or unwillingness) to tax, and from slow productivity growth at home. Global financial integration, moreover, has facilitated the geographical concentration of the ownership of higher value added components of the value chain (e.g. intangible assets and intellectual property) from tangible production. Hence, there is a need to diversify the geographical base on which retirement income is generated, and to capture value where it is most concentrated, or where it is most significantly produced.

Most practically, this means investing in those multinational firms and industries listed on exchanges in the capitals of finance that capture global growth through their leadership of and leverage over global production networks and the innovation process. For the advanced economies of North America, Europe, and East Asia, this means, at least notionally, that capital can stay home or is safely invested in another advanced economy. On the other hand, this means investing in demographically young and rapidly growing emerging economies. But given asymmetric information problems, increased volatility, or potential political instability, investing at this distance is pregnant with risks. This constrains the degree to which capital flows to these economies, even as the barriers to the flow of capital have decreased.

In this chapter we discuss the changing face of the welfare state in the context of the changing geography of production and global financial integration. Although the scope of the welfare state is large in terms of the types of benefits and social guarantees offered, the focus of our attention in this chapter is on the issue of pensions and retirement-income provision, given this inherent link with global finance. The next two sections, Forging the Welfare State, and From Strength to Crisis, describe the historical basis and economic and social foundations of the modern welfare state. We focus specifically on Western European welfare states, given they have been the most advanced in terms of coverage and size relative to GDP, and overall public support.[2] Accordingly, the pronounced shift toward capitalized pension arrangements in Western Europe is significant and revelatory of welfare state development and restructuring elsewhere in terms of coping with the economic risk and uncertainty surrounding demographic aging (Dixon and Sorsa 2009). To provide more specific context, an extended section thereafter— Pension Reform and Global Finance—recounts pension reform in France and policy efforts, particularly the development of a state-sponsored institutional investor, designed to cope with the shifting economic foundations of retirement-income security. While emerging or changing retirement-income arrangements are still conditioned by local institutional conditions and powerful local institutional entrepreneurs, the increasing financialization of retirement-income security nonetheless is contributing to functional convergence across different political economies,

---

[2] For example, in 2012 the average total social expenditure as a percentage of GDP across OECD countries was 21.7. For the pre-2004 European Union enlargement countries, the average was 26.7. See OECD Social Expenditure database.

as they become reliant on and increasingly engaged with financial markets.

Forging the Welfare State

Sharing Risk and Building Nations

The basis for the modern welfare state owes its roots to the development of social insurance in the middle of the nineteenth century. Prior to that, the management of social contingencies (e.g. sickness, old age, and unemployment) occurred through systems of poor relief offered through ecclesiastical or local municipal organizations. The poor and destitute that depended on these organizations, normally without any fault of their own but for the vagaries of social and economic life, were normally stigmatized by society and even stripped of their political and civil rights, to the extent that they had any. With the development of social insurance, risks were pooled together and the individual no longer faced uncertainty alone but as part of a larger group. It was through this aggregation of individuals in a common risk pool—even if such groups were segregated by occupation, religion, and other status distinctions—that the stigmatization of misfortune began to subside. Social insurance reinforced not only the protection and development of one's political and civil rights, but also the beginnings of some basic minimum of protection common to all.

Of the most notable incarnations of social insurance in the nineteenth century were German Chancellor Otto von Bismarck's reforms of the 1880s, which introduced compulsory national insurance against sickness, accidents, old age, and invalidity. Even if the reforms were applied only to and financed mainly by workers, it represented a new stage in the development of the modern state and the relationship between state and citizen (or designated groups therein). As this was a period of nation-state development, Bismarck's reforms had great appeal and were mimicked elsewhere. For instance, Austria-Hungary quickly followed suit establishing insurance schemes for work injuries in 1887 and for sickness in 1888. This was followed by work injury insurance schemes in Norway (1894), Finland (1895), and Italy (1898) (Alber 1981). Such piecemeal development of social insurance continued into the twentieth century, disrupted but not halted by the First World War and then the economic difficulties of the interwar period.

It was not until after the Second World War when the modern welfare state began to take shape, characterized as a state that (1) guarantees individuals and families a minimum income irrespective of the market value of their work or property; (2) narrows the extent of insecurity by enabling individuals and families to meet certain social contingencies; (3) ensures that coverage and access to social services is afforded to all citizens irrespective of status or class (Briggs 1961). It was to the fulfillment of the third objective that the welfare states in Western Europe that developed and expanded in the decades after the Second World War aspired. In one sense the objective was to provide an "optimum" level of services in place of simply a "minimum"; in another sense the objective was to achieve coverage across all members of society. However, the rollout of coverage across all of society differed from country to country. The development of a comprehensive welfare state did not necessarily entail more social solidarity, nor did it necessarily entail a large degree of redistribution.

At the end of the Second World War, the development of social citizenship and solidarity based on principles of universality—wherein the terms of welfare policy included all citizens regardless of class, income, and status distinctions—occurred most prominently in Scandinavian countries and in Great Britain (Marshall 1950). In the latter, for instance, the foundations for a solidaristic welfare state were outlined in the 1942 Beveridge Report, which called for the creation of the National Health Service and the extension of National Insurance (a comprehensive system of social security covering a range of benefits including unemployment, sickness, and retirement) (Harris 1997). The plan for the welfare state outlined in the Beveridge Report would be realized within five years of the war's end with a series of legislative acts. What is key to understanding the developments in Britain and Scandinavia is that while reaching new members of society, such universalistic reforms involved a vertical movement. Benefits and rights that had previously been reserved solely for the poor would now be afforded also to the better off. As a result, a new middle-class interest in social policy was established; they now had a greater stake in the welfare state and its success (Heclo 1974).

In continental Europe, in contrast, Bismarckian social insurance, which attached rights based on group and occupational status, would continue to influence welfare state development after the war. In France and Germany, reformers attempted to introduce universalistic reforms, but were thwarted in their efforts and the separatist approach to social insurance prevailed. This was partly because such efforts to introduce Beveridge-style legislation in these two countries went even further in terms of redistribution than was attempted in Britain and Scandinavia. Groups based on occupational status, mainly the independent professions and salaried employees, were able to resist inclusion into larger risk pools, maintaining instead their individual risk pools. It would not be until the 1960s and 1970s that universalism gained more ground on the continent; economic development began to alter the social distinctions and prospects of different groups, shifting previously reticent groups' support for more redistribution (Baldwin 1990).

Cohesive Communities

Accordingly, the modern welfare states that developed during this period did so based on the logics of "closure" and "membership" (Ferrera 2005). The logic of closure presupposed the existence of a clearly demarcated and cohesive community or communities. At the highest level, community meant the nation-state with its strict political and arguably cultural borders. At lower levels, as in the case of Bismarckian social insurance schemes, community meant a particular occupational or social group. In this nation-state community, and in some cases communities therein, individuals felt or were part of a whole, linked together by reciprocal ties in relation to common risks, such as old age, death, and disability, and common needs, such as healthcare and protection from unseen and difficult economic conditions. But such communities did not mean simply groups of individual citizens.

Community also included other key actors in the economy, particularly national industries and employers. The logic of "membership" meant compulsory or quasi-compulsory association, particularly in public schemes but also frequently in private schemes as well. Together these logics facilitated the institutionalization of pensions and benefits arrangements, with many becoming statutory "social rights." In the case where such arrangements did not become statutory social rights, as in the case of a voluntary occupational pension scheme, their widespread adoption meant, not dissimilarly, that such arrangements became enshrined as social institutions, thus becoming embedded in public and corporate life for a generation (Jacoby 1997). Put simply, the logics of "closure" and "membership" set the framework for defining who would be covered and who would be responsible ultimately for that coverage and the benefits provided—which in most cases meant the nation-state or the firm.

Hence, by the early 1970s different styles of welfare states— or *worlds of welfare* as Gøsta Esping-Andersen (1990) framed them—with characteristic forms of pensions and benefits provision could be discerned. In Anglo-Saxon countries, public pension provision provided a basic safety net, leaving significant scope and need for private market-based provision, which has resulted in large pools of accumulated retirement savings. In continental European countries, pension provision developed on a public or quasi-public basis, with arrangements determined and governed, as in the case of France for example, by occupational affiliation and industry groups. Such arrangements were most often paid for on a pay-as-you-go basis; as a result, private funded arrangements or funded arrangements associated with a single employer or industry association were limited. Scandinavian systems, in contrast, forged universal arrangements based on citizenship and not on occupational status. Unlike the latter, which reinforced different socioeconomic class structures, the Scandinavian systems were designed with significant redistributive elements in them and were largely funded through the tax system.

From Strength to Crisis

The Providence of Reconstruction

Regardless of the form and financing of social policy from country to country, the development of the postwar welfare state occurred in the space of unprecedented economic growth and market expansion. Such high growth supported full employment and provided, moreover, a sound financial and actuarial basis for extending coverage and expanding the range of benefits, whether public or private. Between 1950 and 1970, once Western Europe had regained its footing after the destruction of war, GDP for the region grew 5.5 percent annually on average and 4.4 percent on a per capita basis, compared to the global average of 5 percent and 3 percent respectively. Whereas during the interwar years through to 1950 Europe's place in the global economy had been declining steadily, the 1950s and 1960s would see Western Europe regain some of its industrial strength. During this period Western Europe's share of global output of goods and services increased from 37 percent to 41 percent.

The increase in industrial production would be even larger, increasing from 39 percent to 48 percent. The demographic picture would also help. In comparison to the global average,

Western Europe's population increased at just above half (1.1 percent annually in comparison to 2 percent); by 1970, Western Europe accounted for roughly 26 percent of world population compared with 31 percent in 1950. As population growth remained relatively modest even in the midst of a baby boom, increasing on the range of 1 percent per year, real living standards for most of the population increased significantly (Aldcroft 2001: 128–129). Recall also, as Figure 5.1 shows, old-age dependency ratios were very low during the period. As such, the costs of providing pensions and healthcare to the aged were minimal. With full employment limiting the costs of unemployment insurance, welfare obligations overall were small.

If reconstruction at home provided a major source of growth initially, it would be the structure of the global economy that kept it going. In the 1950s and 1960s the Bretton Woods international monetary system, excluding communist countries and less-developed countries, followed a characteristic core-periphery pattern (Dooley et al. 2004). After the war, as domestic production and infrastructure lay in ruins or were ill equipped, Japan and Europe became heavily reliant on imports of goods and capital for present consumption and reconstruction, much of it coming from the United States. This resulted in significant balance of payments deficits and thus a dollar shortage in those economies. Implementation of the system envisaged at Bretton Woods would turn the situation around by the early 1950s. At the end of 1958 the system was in full force, and for the next 12 years the main European currencies outside the communist world were freely convertible between each other through a fixed exchange rate with the U.S. dollar, fixed and convertible for gold at $35 per ounce. The Japanese yen became fully convertible in 1964. Accordingly, the United States was the center region with essentially uncontrolled capital and goods markets; Western Europe and Japan, whose capital had been destroyed by the war, consisted of the periphery. The center region was used as a financial intermediary that lent credibility to the financial systems of the periphery, lending long term to the periphery, largely through foreign direct investment (FDI), which further stimulated growth through technological diffusion.[3]

What is significant about this arrangement was that the periphery countries were able to follow a development strategy based on undervalued currencies, controls on capital flows and trade, and reserve accumulation. This strategy is much like the pattern of development China is currently following. Thus, for Japan and most Western European countries save the United Kingdom[4], the fixed exchange rate system underpinned export-led growth. But eventually this strategy contributed to a growing and unmanageable U.S. external deficit. The notable contributor to this asymmetry was West Germany, which had become a highly competitive exporter. From the early 1950s the West German economy was consistently in surplus, posing a problem first for the European Payments Union and later the Bretton Woods system. Consequently, the West German government was continually criticized in the Organisation for European Economic Co-operation, the precursor organization to the OECD. The West German government, to its credit, recognized the problem and took steps to alleviate it by liberalizing import policies and by lending modestly abroad. However, this was not sufficient to alter the surplus. The West German government was adamant about addressing the central issues, the Deutsche Mark exchange rate and insufficient domestic demand, for fear of imperiling export-led growth and stoking domestic inflation (Scammell 1980).

Notwithstanding the growth-inducing effects that resulted from this core-periphery development model and progressive market expansion made possible by increasingly liberal trade regimes within Europe and among the other industrialized

[3] The stock of U.S. private direct investment in Europe, for example, increased from 1950 to 1973 by 11.1 percent annually. This contrasts with the period from 1929 to 1950, when U.S. private direct investment in Europe decreased by 1.2 percent annually (Maddison 1991: 153).
[4] For the United Kingdom, in contrast, efforts to sustain sterling as an international reserve currency resulted in periodic balance of payments crises (1947, 1949, 1951, 1955, 1957, 1960–1961, 1964–1965, and 1967–1968).

countries, the relatively unambiguous divide between the "national" and "international" economy would also underwrite the expansion and governance of social policy. Just as the "community" of the nation-state was bordered during this time, so too were the economic capacities of the state. There was a clear basis for long-term planning, or at least the appearance thereof. Nation-state governments and national central banks had more power to engage fiscal and monetary policy to stimulate economic growth, smooth out the business cycle, and therefore, help maintain full employment. As a result, the expansion, governance, and planning of pensions and benefits provision rested on a seemingly stable political–economic platform, where institutions had clear boundaries of responsibility. The institutions charged with providing welfare could be expected to fulfill a certain role in society at certain points in time, thus fortifying the logics of "closure" and "membership."

Elusive Foundations

But soon the economic and actuarial bases of "closure" and "membership" would change. During the 1960s, the U.S. balance of payments deficit would continue to grow, as U.S. overseas FDI continued to expand and the country became embroiled in costly military operations abroad, namely the Vietnam War. Earnings on the U.S. current account were simply too small to cover the outflows. Increased domestic spending, associated with expansion of the U.S. welfare state via President Lyndon Johnson's "Great Society" social policy reforms, would also play a part (Howard 2007). Consequently, U.S. gold reserves declined and surplus dollars held abroad increased significantly. In the last few years of the decade, the U.S. dollar would face a crisis of confidence over its value and its link with gold. The asymmetries in the system became unmanageable. Consequently, between 1970 and 1973, the system of fixed exchange rates based around U.S. dollar convertibility with gold would come to an end, as President Richard Nixon sought to push through a revaluation of the surplus countries' currencies, namely the Deutsche Mark and the yen. This move by the United States represented a major shift in U.S. policy vis-à-vis the international monetary system and the policies it had held constant since the end of the Second World War.[5] At a fundamental level the policy change recognized that the countries of the periphery had graduated to the center in terms of reconstruction and development. Their capital had been rebuilt and their institutions restored. Accordingly, there was no longer a need for a controlled development strategy based on fixed exchange rates for other industrialized countries (Dooley et al. 2004).

Throughout the rest of the 1970s the limits to the postwar development strategy in the industrialized countries revealed themselves further. The exhilarating days of high growth and expanding real income would come to an end. With the economic fallout of global oil price shocks of 1973 and 1979 undermining an increasingly uncertain development path and saturated markets, the 1970s saw intermittent periods of high unemployment, high inflation, and rising social expenditures, which led to large fiscal deficits and an expansion of government debt. The Keynesian policy tools used in previous decades to smooth out the business cycle, facilitate high growth, and limit unemployment, became increasingly ineffectual or only effective temporarily. Industrial progress and the seemingly stable political–economic platform on which the expansion of the welfare state rested had broken down. The economic climate had become harsher and less predictable (Marglin and Schor 1990; Webber and Rigby 1996). The rise of neoliberal economic thought would furthermore question the role of the state in economic affairs as well as the foundations of social solidarity (Glyn 2006; Harvey 2005; Peck 2010).

As might be expected, the growth and development trajectory of pensions and benefits systems began to reverse direction in

[5] For overviews of the rise and fall of the Bretton Woods system, see e.g. Eichengreen (2008), Helleiner (1994), and Strange (1976).

the last two decades of the century (George et al. 2000). Some countries instituted what we can define as paradigmatic reforms where major changes are made to the institutional structure of provision; in other words, we see a major system-wide altera- tion. A well-known example of paradigmatic change is Sweden, where the pension system was partially privatized in 1998 and individual accounts were introduced. In contrast, other coun- tries have instituted parametric reforms—changing the param- eters of benefits provisions—such as increasing the retirement age or lowering the level of benefit, while leaving the basic insti- tutional structures of provision intact. Regardless of the type and scope of reform, capitalization has become a key cornerstone (see also Ebbinghaus 2011). We can examine such parametric development in more depth by considering the case of France.

Pension Reform and Global Finance

Of advanced democracies France is known as having a relatively generous system of social welfare, underpinned by strong repub- lican ideals surrounding social solidarity and the role of the state in society. Such generosity has come at an increasing cost. During the so-called *Trente Glorieuses*, as France's postwar "Golden Age" is referred to, public social spending represented a relatively small part of GDP. Partly in response to worsening economic conditions in the 1970s, social spending increased relatively quickly. The growth in public social spending as a percentage of GDP also reflects the downward or low-growth trajectory of the economy since, which Figure 5.2 helps to visualize. In the figure, the solid line represents the annual rate of GDP growth and the dotted line represents social spending, as a percentage of GDP. Since the 1990s and the early years of this century, however, there has been a relative slowing of public social spending but with- out any significant decrease, not least because of demographic aging. Like other advanced welfare states, France has instituted a number of important reforms to reduce the generosity of the

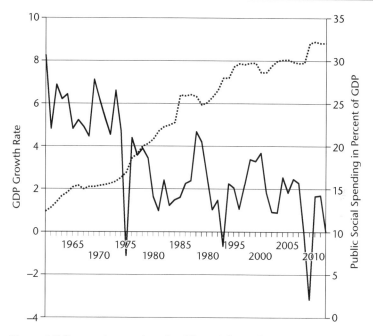

Figure 5.2 Economic growth and public social spending in France, 1960–2012
Source: OECD Social Expenditure database.

welfare state, particularly in the area of pensions. Moreover, there has been a tangible shift away from pay-as-you-go financing to pension benefits reliant on the performance of financial markets.

The Long Road of Reform

Palier and Bonoli (2000) provide a simple schematic for explaining how developments beginning in the 1990s created the environment for the rise of capitalized pension arrangements in advanced industrialized political economies. At the center of their analysis is the argument that pension reform follows particular national paths, given the resilience of inherited institutions and opposition from entrenched interest groups, yet gradually over time moves toward a global model of capitalized

111

pension arrangements. Two conditions have to be met for this to occur. First, the generosity of the pay-as-you-go system must be systematically reduced. Second, a general, though possibly ambiguous, consensus must be reached in both the polity and policymaking community that pre-funding is an acceptable alternative to maintaining the status quo. Though they do not give an indication of what new funded institutions will look like, the important feature is that pay-as-you-go arrangements will be increasingly replaced by pre-funded ones or some degree thereof. This schematic precisely follows changes in France.

The French pension system is a complex fragmented structure made up of first pillar and quasi-public second pillar pay-as-you-go regimes, which has made it difficult for efforts to reform the system.[6] The basic *régime général*, which was introduced in 1946, covers private sector workers, who are then also covered by complementary pay-as-you-go regimes on a sectoral basis. The latter are managed by the representative councils: the *Association générale des institutions de retraite complémentaire des cadres* (AGIRC) and the *Association pour le régime de retraite complémentaire des salariés* (ARRCO). Public sector workers are covered by their own pay-as-you-go regimes. This somewhat limited state role, in that the pension system is partially decentralized, has strong historical roots. Many sector-based associations had already long established themselves in the provision from as early as the nineteenth century. Hence, in the initial postwar years the Gaullist government promoted the extension of the complementary regimes (Whiteside 2006).

Despite the difficulty of reforming the system, reforms have been introduced. The future viability of the French system has long been an important issue in France since the late-1980s. The first major pension reform in France came in 1993 after years of public debate and government commissioned reports over the

---

[6] In general discussion first pillar refers to mandatory state pension regimes, second pillar refers to employer-sponsored occupational pensions, and third pillar refers to individual pensions. See World Bank (1994).

future health of the French pension system. With important concessions made to trade unions, the Balladur government, a coalition of the center-right UDF (Union for French Democracy) and RPR (Rally for the Republic) parties, successfully pushed through a set of important changes. However, these reforms were limited to the *régime général* and not the public sector *régimes spéciaux*. Three important benefit-reducing alterations occurred with this reform. First, the number of contribution years necessary to receive the full retirement benefit increased from 37.5 years to 40 years. Second, the reference wage for determining the benefit would be derived from the best 25 years instead of the best ten years. Third, the indexation of pensions would follow the evolution of prices and not the evolution of wages (Palier 2003).

In 2003 the center-right coalition regained control of the government and proceeded to enact further pension reforms with the *loi Fillon*. The major outcome of the *loi Fillon* was the increase in the contribution period for a full benefit for the public functionaries' scheme from 37.5 to 40 years. The contribution period for both the functionaries' scheme and private sector schemes would progressively increase to 41 years by 2012, and pensions would be indexed based on prices and not on the evolution of wages. In addition, the *loi Fillon* created two pension savings vehicles, the *Plan d'épargne pour la retraite populaire* and the *Plan d'épargne retraite collectif*. The former is an individual pension scheme where contributions are tax deductible to a certain limit. The latter is a collective occupational pension scheme allowing for both employee and employer contributions with certain tax advantages.[7]

In 2010 the center-right government again pushed through further pension reforms, as recession and increased unemployment further strained the viability of the system, which had a deficit of €32 billion. The main part of the reform was an increase in the legal retirement age from 60 to 62, with the

---

[7] "Loi n° 2003-775 du 21 août 2003 portant réforme des retraites" *Journal Officiel de la République Française.*

age necessary to receive the full pension benefit increasing from 65 to 67.[8] If the first condition of Palier and Bonoli's hypothesis, the expansion of funded options through a diminution of pay-as-you-go arrangements, had already occurred for most French citizens with the 2003 reforms, the 2010 reform thus reinforced the trend.

The second condition—that of increasing the consensus surrounding funded pensions as an acceptable alternative—is equally important. The financial portfolio of French households from the national financial accounts is a viable proxy for judging this.[9] For example, in 1977 just 4 percent of French households' financial assets were held in life insurance and pension savings products. By 2009, life insurance and pension savings products represented 42 percent of financial assets, as shown in Figure 5.3.[10] In France, life insurance, known as *assurance-vie*, generally provides payment in the case of death before a particular date, or a payment in capital or annuity after the assured reaches a certain age. Hence, *assurance-vie*, which comes with fiscal advantages, functions as a retirement-savings product.

Such a substantial increase in French households' holdings of retirement-savings products since the early 1990s suggests that French households became more concerned with their financial health at retirement, as the generosity of the pay-as-you-go system started to decrease; pension reforms forced French households to pay more attention to their retirement security.[11] At the same time, it could be argued that French households lost some of their faith in the long-term viability of the pay-as-you-go

[8] "Loi n° 2010-1330 du 9 novembre 2010 portant réforme des retraites" *Journal Officiel de la République Française.*

[9] Data in Figure 5.3 are taken from the June 9, 2010 version of long time series of annual national financial accounts compiled by the *Banque de France*, which uses the European System of Accounts 95 classifications.

[10] Prior to 1985 French households' financial portfolio were held primarily in traditional savings accounts and fixed-term deposits. In addition to the growth of life insurance and pension savings, French households likewise increased their holdings of equities and mutual funds (UCITS), while holdings of bonds decreased.

[11] This also demonstrates the emergence of a more market-based financial system.

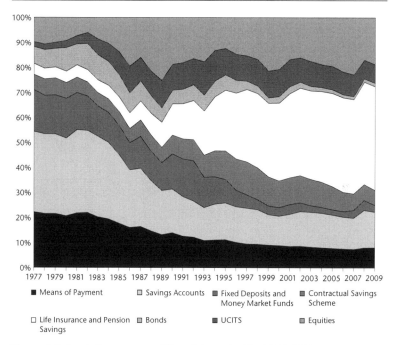

Figure 5.3 Portfolio structure of French households, 1977–2009

Source: Banque de France, National Financial Accounts.

system. What is important, regardless, is that funded retirement has become clearly embedded in both statute and the outlook of French citizens. But even in the face of increasing privatization and individualization of retirement-income security, the state still seeks an active role.

In the Shadow of Dirigisme

Comparative social scientists have long held that France is typified as "state-led" or "statist" capitalism (see e.g. Shonfield 1965). In the postwar period, the French state became the key actor in French economic and industrial reconstruction and a key owner of French industry and commerce. Beginning in the 1970s, the state-led tradition of economic governance, also known as *dirigisme*, began to unravel. Macroeconomic management became restricted and limited, as Bretton Woods fell apart and the European Monetary System began to emerge. For industry, global competition rendered less viable the practice of picking and supporting "national champions." Internally, the institutional centralization of political–economic power in Paris at the expense of local and societal organizations seemed ill equipped to respond to the new global environment. In the early 1980s, the Socialist-led Mitterrand government began to reorient government policy increasingly toward the market by liberalizing aspects of the financial system, granting increasing autonomy to managers, adopting more orthodox monetary policies, and discontinuing support for failing companies. Postwar *dirigisme* had effectively come to an end (Levy 1999). Despite the end to a "strong" type of *dirigisme* in the 1980s, some scholars argue that the state continues to play a major role in the French political economy. For Schmidt (2002, 2003), France's postwar "state-led" capitalism has evolved into what can be called "state-enhanced" capitalism, wherein the state continues to exercise significant albeit less direct influence, in comparison to its highly directive role in the past (Clift 2006; Levy 2006).

Even if the strong form of *dirigisme* has long been abandoned, it arguably gives expression and direction to policymaking and actions. *Dirigisme* may not necessarily embody a regulative institution; it is, rather, a recurrent normative and discursive institution.[12] In this sense *dirigisme* might not always appear as an active policy commitment of coercing economic behavior to a certain direction. It is more likely that *dirigisme* is found in the state setting norms concerning and using authority over economic behavior (Dixon and Sorsa 2009). State-led actions may also be understood as an effective schema to start promoting societal change. The idea of state-led action and solutions is in

---

[12] Regulative institutions, such as rules and laws, define what agents may and may not do. Normative institutions, such as values and expectations, define what agents should and should not do, thus providing legitimacy to actions. Discursive (or cognitive–cultural) institutions define what is and is not true, and what can and cannot be done (see Scott 2008).

this sense based on shared understanding and is thus less susceptible to contestation whatever the particular norms behind it at any period of time.

Although it may appear that pension reform has been limited to the center-right, the socialist Jospin government (1997–2002) did much to keep the issue of pension reform and the insecurity of the pension system at the forefront of debate by commissioning several reports. Moreover, the Jospin government sought to protect the pay-as-you-go pension system through partial pre-funding by passing legislation in 1998 for a government pension reserve fund with an initial contribution of 2 billion francs as part of the 1999 "*loi de financement de la sécurité sociale.*" These funds would be invested in financial markets and managed by the government as a separate accounting section of the *Fonds de solidarité vieillesse*—a fund that ensures the financing of various non-contributory benefits relevant to social solidarity, primarily in the *minimum vieillesse*—a basic income support scheme for pensioners without other and/or inadequate retirement income.

In July 2001 the mandate of the pension reserve fund was modified from its mainly symbolic beginning in 1999, naming it the *Fonds de réserve pour les retraites* (FRR) and transforming it into an autonomous state agency, considering the mission of the fund and the significant size of the asset pool it would manage over time. Specifically, the fund would accumulate reserves until 2020. These funds would come from a variety of sources, such as state privatizations. The accumulated reserves would then be used to smooth the effects of demographic aging on the pay-as-you-go system until 2040. The reformed mandate also set up a governing body consisting of members of parliament, members of government, and the social partners. In other words, the new governance system is autonomous but its composition is derived primarily from the national political system. Furthermore, the administration and custodianship of the FRR was granted to the state-controlled financial institution the *Caisse des dépôts*. In terms of financial management, the reform directed the fund to auction funds to private sector asset managers through a competitive bid process.

The creation of the FRR indicates a willingness of the French state to maintain a strong presence in retirement-income provision even when provision is relying on the performance of global financial markets. Indeed, the French government could have left pre-funding exclusively to second and third pillar schemes as many pension systems do. This resonates with the "state enhancement" thesis regarding France. On the one hand, recent reforms have normatively and substantively increased private solutions to pension provision. On the other hand, the state has "enhanced" the national first pillar with a public solution that seems reminiscent of its *dirigiste* past.

A Global Investor

Though the creation of the FRR elicits overtones of *dirigisme*, the structure and scope of the FRR as a global institutional investor is a classic case of institutional *translation*. On one level public pension reserve funds have been utilized by governments for some time to partially fund pay-as-you-go social security systems, such as exists in Canada for instance. In this sense the government borrowed a practice utilized by others, yet translated it to the particularities of its own system (Djelic and Quack 2007; see also Gertler 2004). On another level the FRR appears to embody the practices and institutional scope of other large global institutional investors, at least in its initial development prior to the financial crisis. This can be seen in its asset allocation and organizational structure.

Asset allocation is the single most important factor affecting total return and performance (Brinson et al. 1991). A less than optimal asset allocation, the balance between risk and return, could be detrimental to the welfare of beneficiaries. Accordingly, optimizing asset allocation is fundamental to and characteristic of sophisticated global pension funds and institutional investors. At the end of 2006 the FRR had 26.4 percent of its

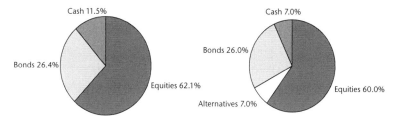

Figure 5.4 Global average asset allocation, 2006

Source: FRR Annual Report 2006, Watson Wyatt 2007 Global Pension Assets Study.

assets in bonds, 62.1 percent in equities, and 11.5 percent in cash and other money market securities. This asset allocation is comparable, as visualized in Figure 5.4, to other global pension funds. A study by the professional services consultancy Watson Wyatt (now Towers Watson) showed that at the end of 2006 the aggregate asset allocation of pension funds globally was 60 percent in equities, 26 percent in bonds, and the remaining 14 percent divided roughly in half between cash and alternative investments.

Like the FRR, these comparable institutions have relatively long investment horizons given the nature of their liabilities. The investment horizon is an important factor when considering a fund's strategic asset allocation and why long-term institutional investors generally favor equities over fixed-income securities. Using the S&P 500 index (SPX) and its antecedents, Fama and French (2002) estimate that the average real return for the index from 1872 to 2000 was 8.81 percent. The average real return for six-month commercial paper, a proxy for the risk-free interest rate, was 3.24 percent. As such, the equity premium over the course of more than a century was 5.57 percent (see also Dimson et al. 2002).

Considering the similarity in asset allocation between the FRR and the global average, it is reasonable to argue that the FRR is modeling its investment strategy, and therefore the institution itself, on other global pension funds. To effectuate such an investment strategy requires a certain degree of institutional sophistication, or at least a capacity to delegate this strategy externally to a competitive market of consultants and asset managers. In other words, investing at the institutional level requires at least a minimum of sophistication of financial practice and organizational structure to move such large sums of money in and between markets and asset classes (Davis and Steil 2001). The organizational structure of the FRR appears to fulfill this requirement. Within the FRR organization there is a dedicated finance department divided into an investment strategy and risk management division, a tactical asset allocation division, a division to monitor its external asset managers, and a middle office for reporting. Furthermore, the FRR has a separate unit that monitors investment performance. To be sure, the FRR is not a constrained state bureaucracy.

Where the FRR diverged in comparison with the global aggregate asset allocation of pension funds, is investment in alternatives (private equity, real estate, commodities, and infrastructure). These alternative investments can be an important part of risk diversification beyond equities and fixed income as well as a source of added value for long-term investors (Campbell and Viceira 2002). As such, the diversification and possible higher rates of return from alternative asset classes suggests that sophisticated institutional investors would include a portion of these in their asset allocations. In May 2006 the FRR released a strategic allocation plan, i.e. future investment targets, with a goal of placing 60 percent of assets in equities, 30 percent in bonds, and 10 percent in alternative assets.[13] This allocation would have firmly placed the FRR, with a 70/30 equity and equity-type investment to bond allocation, comparable to the conventional global pension fund asset allocation at that time.

The global financial crisis and the ensuing economic recession would, however, alter the course of the FRR's investment

---

[13] FRR Supervisory Board Resolution May 2006.

strategy. Given the significant degradation of the receipts to the *Fonds de solidarité vieillesse* as a consequence of the recession, the 2010 pension reform altered the mission of the FRR significantly. Instead of accumulating capital until 2020 and then drawing down the fund through 2040, the FRR beginning in 2011 would pay €2.1 billion annually through 2024 to the *Caisse d'amortissement de la dette sociale*, which is charged with redeeming and amortizing social security deficits, to help finance deficits of the *Fonds de solidarité vieillesse*, and an estimated one-off payment in 2020 of €3.4 billion to the *Caisse national de l'assurance vieillesse*, which manages the *régime général*. The annual endowments the FRR had received until 2010 would thenceforth go directly to the *Caisse d'amortissement de la dette sociale*.

Yet crisis, recession, and a fundamental change in mission would not change the FRR's long-term outlook regarding the prospects and possibilities of global financial markets and the organization's commitment to achieving sophistication. In December 2010, the supervisory board of the FRR, in following the dictates of the new pension reform, adopted a liability-driven investment model and split the roughly €35 billion portfolio into two components: a performance component comprising equities, higher risk bonds, and alternative assets; and a hedging component comprising cash and fixed-income products. Consequently, by splitting the portfolio into two components the FRR is supposed to be able to cover the new short- to medium-term liabilities set by the new law with the hedging component but still achieve potentially higher rates of return over the long term from the performance component by taking more risk. At the end of 2012 the performance component accounted for 41.4 percent of assets against 58.6 percent in the hedging component, as shown in Figure 5.5. While the FRR supervisory board had to effectively flip the pre-crisis conventional asset allocation on its head given its new investment time horizon, the global financial crisis did little to undermine the FRR as a global investor.

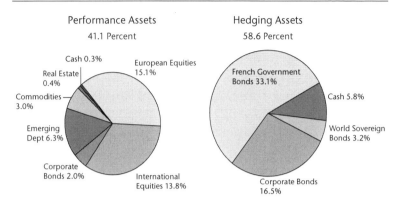

Figure 5.5 Asset allocation of the *Fonds de réserve pour les retraites*, 2012
Source: Fonds de réserve pour les retraites.

Conclusions

What high economic growth, full employment, and a demographically young population structure meant for the development of the welfare state after the Second World War, was that these factors provided a sound financial and actuarial basis for extending coverage and expanding the range of benefits, whether public or private. This is not to imply that the welfare state and economic policy did not make a material contribution to sustaining high economic growth by ensuring a healthy and committed workforce and a confident consumer market. Nor does this imply that public policy was not crucial in supporting full employment. Even if the political and social impetus for instituting the welfare state was strong and necessary, the economic conditions provided by reconstruction both at home and abroad could not be more favorable. But, structural foundations change.

Demographic aging, low economic growth, high unemployment, constrained government budgets, and the emergence of "new social risks" pose critical challenges to advanced welfare states in the beginning of the twenty-first century (Nyce and Schieber 2005; Taylor-Gooby 2004). In response, all European countries have instituted some type of pension reform, effectively reducing the size of the non-funded component of the overall pension contract, and paving the way for new capitalized retirement-income institutions and the transformation of old ones (Queisser et al. 2007; Whiteford and Whitehouse 2006). The creation of partially or fully funded pension systems has one important implication: they create massive pools of retirement savings housed in an array of retirement-income institutions (e.g., pension funds, mutual funds, banks, and insurance companies) whose influence is being felt in every capital market in the world.

What the adoption of capitalized retirement-income arrangements means is that pension provision is transferred to the domain of finance, to specific institutions of finance and actor networks of the financial community. On the surface, the turn toward global finance is where political–economic convergence lies. There are various interpretations of this shift. For some, it illustrates a potentially more sustainable means of pension provision and source of solidarity compared to nation-states, providing a clearer solution to demographic aging and a means of promoting economic growth by developing local and global capital markets (Holzmann and Hinz 2005). Some argue that pension asset pools provide a means to take control over the means of production, especially or only if fiduciary regulations are adjusted. But some remain more skeptical about this (for a review, see Langley 2008). For others, it represents "Ponzi finance" distorting the financial system and constantly disturbing the real economy, as growing amounts of contributions flood the market and thus alter corporate finance and banking activity (Toporowski 2000); it illustrates "grey accumulation" of capital that increases financial fragility and possibly enhancing pension crises (Blackburn 2006).

Although pension systems in Europe remain institutionally diverse, with different levels of public and private involvement, the utilization of common financial logics that transcend political–economic boundaries by local retirement-income institutions has important implications for understanding political–economic diversity and institutional change. Indeed, investment practice and financial services have taken on a language of their own that appears to transcend many institutional and political–economic differences (Froud et al. 2007). Investment banks, asset managers, pension funds, and insurance companies across Europe increasingly operate in global markets in tandem with and under similar logics, such as modern portfolio theory and expectations of financial performance, as their Anglo-American counterparts (Knorr-Cetina and Preda 2005). This is clearly evidenced in the case of the FRR.

Even if the general outcome of pension reform is similar—an increasing reliance on and integration with global financial markets—the past institutional setting weighs on the design of new institutions. Diversity among different institutional settings suggests that different option-sets exist within which some options outweigh others (Pierson 2004). Rarely do reformers—the various actors or cohorts of actors operating in economic, social, or political spheres that drive change—work with a blank slate. This limits the degree of convergence on a common institutional design, thus providing continued scope for formal diversity. It also limits the outright dismantling of the welfare state—increasing financialization does not necessarily signify deep retrenchment. In effect, although strong links with global finance are made, retirement-income arrangements remain embedded in and steered by the regulative, normative, and discursive institutional environments of the political economy in question. The strong state-led response in France, which has been coupled with wider reform efforts to encourage individual retirement planning and savings, is such an example. Regardless of persistent local differences, functional similarity and thus institutional convergence is noticeably manifest.

6

Corporate Transformation
and Employee Pensions

For a number of advanced democracies, firms, alongside the nation-state, have had an important place in the provision of social insurance. In the United States, for example, supplementary employer-sponsored pension schemes became a cornerstone of retirement-income security (Ghilarducci 1992; Sass 1997). These likewise became conventional in countries such as Canada, the United Kingdom, Japan, Switzerland, the Netherlands, and Finland. While espousing a different form from public pensions, the function of occupational pensions, in terms of benefit formulae, would be the same: to provide beneficiaries a guaranteed income in retirement. In general, the employer, and in some cases the employee, paid contributions into these defined benefit pension plans. Crucially, the employer bore the entire responsibility of covering the predefined retirement income of the employee regardless of life expectancy and the investment performance of the pension fund.

Beginning in the 1990s the defined benefit pension as a part of the wage and benefits package for employees began to lose favor with employers. Instead, employers started to favor pension schemes that followed a defined contribution formula, if they had not shied away from offering retirement benefits at all (Munnell and Sunden 2004). Under the latter package, the employee and the employer generally contribute to the plan jointly, of which the employer or the employee, depending on the arrangement, decides investments. Yet, unlike defined benefit schemes, the employer absolves itself from the risk that the accumulated retirement savings will be inadequate due to poor investment performance and/or higher than anticipated life expectancy.

The demise of the corporate-sponsored defined benefit pension can be attributed largely to the changing form and function of the modern firm.[1] The zenith of the defined benefit pension occurred during the decades following the Second World War, when corporate form and function was dominated by the vertically integrated conglomerate, where internal labor markets, bank-based finance and reinvestment of earnings, dominated convention. With rapid technological change, expanding global markets and opportunities for offshoring and outsourcing, and efforts to extract value from firms through financial market actions (e.g. divestitures and leveraged buyouts), corporate form and function assumes a variety of shapes, both in terms of geographical scope and intra-firm management techniques. Victim to this shift from the so-called "old" economy based on industrial manufacturing to a "new" economy based on advanced technology and knowledge-based services has been the defined benefit pension. It has become a long-term liability many firms are no longer willing to assume (Monk 2008, 2009b). Many firms no longer see the benefit of providing defined benefit pensions, regardless of whether or not there may be value-generating outcomes through the retention of highly skilled employees (Lazear 1990).

Two other considerations should be noted in addition to changing corporate forms behind the gradual individualization of occupational retirement benefits: changing political

---

[1] Public-employee pension schemes in general have been more resilient than private-sector pension schemes, but even they have seen significant retrenchment and reform.

economies; and changing work patterns. Engelen (2006) attributes the rise of occupational defined benefit pensions (in conjunction with the welfare state in general) to post-Second World War industrialization, but emphasizes the general social constitution of the period. The model of social and economic reproduction in almost every advanced political economy at the time was characterized by the nuclear family, headed by a full-time, fully tenured male breadwinner. As such, the insurance provided by the firm was based on the assumption of high levels of homogeneity among those insured (the male breadwinner and his family), stable employment relations, and low job mobility. In other words, there was a high level of continuity and perceived stability, where risks were exogenous and calculable.

If the success of vertical redistribution called for pension plans with a level of solidarity among workers that share similar socioeconomic risks, this is less the case now. In the last several decades, almost all advanced political economies have seen increased deindustrialization in terms of the proportion of workers in industrial employment, with increasing proportions working in the services sector. Accompanying such structural economic change has been an increase in job mobility along with atypical and precarious employment patterns, together with a substantial increase in female labor-force participation. Hence, the actuarial basis on which sound funding principles rely has become more complex and uncertain. These changes, including significant increases in life expectancy, destabilized (if the typical postwar political economy was actually ever stable) the post-Second World War modes, both public and private, of occupational welfare provision.

The shift to more flexible arrangements, such as the defined contribution pension, is in theory supposed to accommodate these changing occupational conditions and shifting boundary demarcations. Defined contribution schemes are supposed to suit firms that need flexibility or themselves may have a short lifespan given technological or economic change. Defined contribution schemes are also supposed to support the mobile worker, who may change jobs multiple times and who lacks any strong commitment to either similar workers or a single firm. Whatever specifics can be drawn, the shift is ultimately a recognition that firms are less embedded in any particular place. The globalization of finance and the globalization of supply chains have liberated the firm from its history and geography; they are geographical solutions to the embedded firm.

Whereas previous modes of provision relied heavily on a sense of shared expectations, whether among workers of a firm or workers/citizens of a particular nation-state, this is less so the case now in occupational pension provision. New modes of occupational pension provision leave little by way of social solidarity, and to the relationship firms have with individuals and society at large, beyond the immediate employment relationship. However, the degree, the speed, and the form of individualization are often contingent on the particular political economy in question. Yet, no matter the context, private firms have been able to discharge responsibility for the long-term well-being of their employees.

Assessment of this change is made initially in the first section, From Old Economy to New Economy, where we analyze the evolution of the components of the Dow Jones Industrial Average (DJIA) from just after the height of the postwar economic boom in the mid-1970s to the contemporary period. Even though the DJIA index concerns U.S. multinationals, it serves as a proxy for decomposing the changing landscape and long-term commitments of firms more generally in the shift from "old" economy to "new" economy firms, given its historic role as the oldest continuing index and as a benchmark for large corporate securities and equity markets worldwide. Its small size of only 30 constituents also simplifies the illustration. We then consider in the section, En Route to a Global Standard, the changing conditions and expectations of global financial markets, which have been expressed through modifications in accounting standards and their international harmonization. In recent years, changes in accounting standards, particularly the adoption of the fair value method, have either catalyzed the transformation of the corporate-sponsored defined benefit pension or simply reinforced its decline.

The section Veiled Convergence, compares and contrasts the changing environment of occupational pension provision in the United Kingdom and the Netherlands. Whereas the United Kingdom has seen a massive decline in occupational defined benefit pension coverage, the Netherlands has managed to renegotiate the defined benefit pension promise in such a way that facilitates flexibility and shares risk among members of the pension scheme. However, as in the United Kingdom, firms have successfully reduced their long-term risk exposure by limiting their liability. But the decline of the defined benefit pension in the United Kingdom does not mean there has been a triumph of neoliberalism. The United Kingdom is actually converging closer to the Dutch model, with the state having mandated, with the 2008 Pensions Act, that firms enroll their employees in an occupational pension scheme or the new National Employment Savings Trust. Nonetheless, this does not mean that firms are mandated to take on long-term pension liabilities. Ultimately, while the decline of defined benefit pensions in both countries has been significant, the transformation remains somewhat differentiated but still similar. Even in places with seemingly strong foundations of social solidarity, firms are increasingly abdicating responsibility for the long-term welfare of their employees.

From "Old" Economy to "New" Economy

Whereas for most of the twentieth century stock markets were dominated by large asset-intensive vertically integrated industrial conglomerates, the landscape of large firms is now more heterogeneous, with many more services-oriented and human-capital-intensive firms. Understanding this evolution is important for three reasons. First, the vertically integrated industrial conglomerates that developed over the postwar years were the primary sponsors of private sector defined benefit pensions. As the strength and importance of these firms have declined, so has pension coverage. Second, the lifespan of firms can change or end rapidly as the context in which the firm operates changes. Some firms that once figured prominently have ceased to exist. This has important implications for the maintenance of the firm's pension liabilities, especially as obligations increase with demographic aging. Third, competitors without long-term liabilities can challenge the market position of seasoned firms with extensive liabilities, as the former has more flexibility in employing capital and raising new capital.

In evaluating the component list of the DJIA at four different points and whether the firms provided defined benefit pensions, we can document this shift. Each point represents the date of a change to the constituent list; the points are spaced roughly a decade apart, save for the last point. Firms are classified using the Industry Classification Benchmark, and information of pension schemes was obtained from U.S. Department of Labor Form 5500 filings, corporate annual reports, and corporate press releases.

The Apex of Vertically Integrated Firms

The first chart in Figure 6.1 shows the sector composition of the DJIA as of September 1976, at arguably the peak of the post-Second World War corporate order just before the major corporate restructurings that swept U.S. capital markets during the 1980s (Jensen 1993). Prior to August 1976, other than with the addition of Chrysler, the index had not changed since 1959, which demonstrates the stability of the period. The index was clearly dominated by vertically integrated industrial and basic materials companies, with nine and eight members respectively. These included such notables as U.S. Steel, Bethlehem Steel, Inco, International Harvester, and General Electric. General Motors and Chrysler, classified under consumer goods, were the two automobile manufacturers of the index. Unlike today,

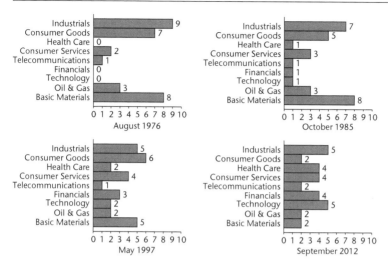

Figure 6.1 Dow Jones Industrial Average historical components
Source: Dow Jones Indexes.

not one financial services firm, technology firm, or pharmaceuticals firm (healthcare) is listed. The one telecommunications firm was AT&T, which had a monopoly on telephone service in the United States until 1982, when regulators broke the company up. At this time, all of the firms on the index offered a defined benefit pension plan to at least some if not most of their employees.

The Start of High-tech and Financials

Looking at the index nearly a decade later in October 1985, we see the beginnings of a decline in the economic significance of heavy industry. IBM and Merck & Co. were added in 1979, becoming, respectively, the first technology and healthcare firms to enter the index. American Express was added in 1982, becoming the first financial services firm on the index. The McDonald's Corporation joined in 1985. The members of the basic materials component of the index remained the same. Johns-Manville, an asbestos and industrial materials producer,

131

had been removed from the index in 1979; it simultaneously filed for bankruptcy protection following class-action lawsuits related to asbestos claims. Chrysler had been removed in 1979 leaving General Motors as the only automobile producer on the index. This was a turning point for North American automobile manufacturing as it marked the important effects of global competition, mainly from Japan, on firm competitiveness (see Schoenberger 1997). In terms of pension provision, the new entrants to the list sponsored defined benefit pensions plans, save for the McDonald's Corporation. The shift from basic materials and industrials did not necessarily entail a change in the outlook of firms with regard to long-term pension liabilities.

Nearing the "New" Economy

Moving ahead 12 years to May 1997, just before the dot-com stock market bubble, we see that the transition from "old" to "new" economy firms had shifted even more. Basic materials and industrials had moved from a total of 17 in 1976 to only ten by 1997. Both steel producers on the index had been removed, as were American Can, International Harvester, and Owens-Illinois Glass. American Can became Primerica Corporation in 1987, after having transformed itself from a manufacturing firm into a financial services firm. Hewlett-Packard joined IBM in the technology sector; Travelers Group and J.P. Morgan & Co. joined American Express in financials; Johnson & Johnson joined Merck & Co. in healthcare; and, in consumer services, The Walt Disney Company, the first media company on the index, joined Sears Roebuck & Company, and McDonalds. Clearly by this time traditional manufacturing's moment as a focal point of value creation had come to an end. American Can's transformation into a financial services firm exemplifies this shift. Although the shift in the index away from heavy industry was significant, many companies, even those associated with the "new" economy, still continued to offer defined benefit pension plans. Of the new entrants during the period, only Wal-Mart Stores, Inc. did not offer a defined benefit plan.

The End of Defined Benefit

In the first decade of the twenty-first century the composition of the index shifted further toward "new economy" firms. The bankruptcy of General Motors and its subsequent removal from the index in June 2009 highlights this shift. While not the only problem facing the company, its long-term obligations to employee pensions and healthcare costs were at the center of the bankruptcy. Some of the new entrants during the period, such as Microsoft and Cisco Systems in the technology sector, and Home Depot in consumer services, never offered defined benefit pension schemes. For the rest of the index, the "perfect storm" of low interest rates and inadequate investment returns following the dot-com bubble, coupled with increasing beneficiary longevity, vastly increased pension costs. The subprime crisis produced another "perfect storm". Consequently, most firms on the index have closed their defined benefit pensions or have converted them into cash balance plans, which create hypothetical accounts for each employee much like a defined contribution plan. As of end of 2012, only two companies on the index offered defined benefit plans to a broad range of employees. Some firms still maintain defined benefit plans, but only for select employees. The policy of providing guaranteed retirement benefits is, ultimately, no longer a convention.

En Route to a Global Standard

If the costs associated with demographic aging coupled with structural changes to the global economy are the primary drivers behind the decline of defined benefit pensions, changes to how firms account for and disclose long-term pension obligations has helped catalyze the change. The harmonization of accounting standards across the globe in the last decade has meant that such changes are not limited to only a few countries.

On January 1, 2005, all listed companies in the European Union began using the International Accounting Standards Board's (IASB) International Financial Reporting Standards (IFRS), which also includes International Accounting Standards (IAS). The IASB and the U.S. Financial Accounting Standards Board (FASB), which produces Statements of Financial Accounting Standards (SFAS), have been in negotiations since October 2004 to develop a common conceptual framework that builds on their own existing frameworks. Other national accounting standards boards have also answered the call for convergence. For instance, since 2005 the Accounting Standards Board of Japan and the IASB have been working to eliminate differences between Japanese Generally Accepted Accounting Practices (GAAP) and IFRS. The Accounting Standards Board of Canada formally adopted IFRS in 2011. Singapore, Russia, Turkey, and Australia have also been moving toward increased convergence with IFRS along with countless other countries, either through formal adoption or setting equivalent standards. What is more, in countries where convergence is not currently underway to a significant extent, many large firms already report in IFRS or U.S. GAAP in addition to local standards, because they are either cross-listed on major stock exchanges in the United States or Europe, or because they actively seek international investment capital. In effect, it is difficult to find an economy or major firm not subject in some way or another to the process of accounting harmonization.

The objective of accounting standards harmonization is to facilitate investment decision-making and the allocation of capital at a global scale, by improving the consistency, comparability, and continuity of financial reporting. Consistency of information facilitates scoring and summation. Comparability of information allows institutional investors to weigh investment opportunities across industries and jurisdictions, which puts the emphasis on the specific characteristics of the firm. For example, this facilitates pricing firms with, versus firms without, defined benefit pension obligations. Continuity of information also allows for the comparison of investment opportunities between different periods in time. Standardization thus facilitates the spread of institutional investment across countries, and hence the influence of conventional logics running through financial markets.

Finding Fair Value

Concurrent to accounting standards harmonization has been the move toward fair value accounting. Fair value accounting records asset values at the going spot market price (i.e. "marking to market"). Where traded market values do not exist for a particular asset, then a model of the flows generated by the asset is made. For the accounting standards boards, fair value offers a more objective and faithful view of the firm by uncovering the true value of assets and liabilities. In effect, this should, in their view, also provide a more accurate assessment of a firm's current and future risks. Finally, by using spot market values, fair value is supposed to facilitate external monitoring by shareholders and financial market analysts, as it limits the room for flexibility in the drawing up of income and other measures in financial statements (Bignon et al. 2004).

Critics argue, however, that fair value is fundamentally flawed given its reliance on the Efficient Markets Hypothesis, which assumes that investors are fully rational and adjust their decisions without cost following price signals (Whittington 2008). In the real world, markets are often not efficient, markets may at times seem irrational, and transaction costs can be significant. Consequently, prices are not necessarily a true and accurate reflection of value and risk. Furthermore, fair value models, used in the absence of spot markets, are also problematic due to potential manipulation, as was demonstrated by the Enron Corporation's fraudulent accounting, which ultimately resulted in one of the largest corporate bankruptcies in U.S. history (Benston 2006).

At the same time, although fair value claims to more accurately reflect "current" values, it inherently relies on "future" values, which themselves are ultimately unknowable and based on subjective criteria. As such, rather than representing a truly objective form of accountancy, we may simply be witnessing a shift in the subjective decision-making from one agent (the firm) to another agent (the regulator or the shareholder). This raises an important question about fair value accounting: fair to whom? While refraining from making an explicit value judgment on the merits or demerits of fair value accounting over other methods, we may contend, more importantly, that accounting is not a simple objective and technical exercise. As Mouck (2004) argues, following Searle's (1995) institutional reality and without adhering to more complete social constructivist accounting perspectives, financial accounting representations are epistemologically objective in that they can only come into existence with a set of rules, which themselves have no objective basis in either physical or institutional reality. Accounting standardization around any particular paradigm is therefore inherently political, where the interests of some may come to dominate the interests of others—e.g. management versus labor, or shareholders versus management. There is the possibility, then, of unexplored impacts of accounting on different stakeholders and the public at large (Biondi and Suzuki 2007).

Accounting for Old Age

Pension accounting specifically is part of this broad-based shift to fair value. Both IAS 19 and SFAS 158, which are accounting standards for pension obligations, follow a fair value approach. Under fair value significant market fluctuations in pension plan asset values introduce considerable volatility up or down into a firm's balance sheet, which are reported to the market in the firm's quarterly and annual reports. In effect, fair value redirects short-term fluctuations in the pension funds (which are by their very nature long-term institutions) directly into short-term corporate financial statements (Boyer 2007). Accordingly, a significant market downturn may cause a significant cost to the firm as it shifts resources to cover pension obligations even though the downturn may only be a short-term event in relative terms to the long-term time horizon of the pension obligation.[2]

As Rauh (2006) demonstrates, actions to rectify funding deficits can have a negative effect on capital expenditures, which can translate into missed investment and market opportunities to competing firms leaving the firm in a worse-off position in the long term. As a result, how these pension plan deficits are calculated and reported is of vital importance for corporate performance and valuation. In a world in which pension deficits are calculated according to "fair value" on a quarterly basis, it may seem obvious that firms would shy away from providing defined benefit pensions when at all possible. Yet, a situation such as this may have been avoided under alternative smoothing mechanisms of previous accounting rules where periods of market volatility did not make it into the balance sheet. Interestingly, other research has shown that fair value pension accounting may not be an improvement on previous disclosure and accounting rules since it impairs value and credit relevance of financial statements unless transitory gains and losses, i.e. the short-term ups and downs of asset values are separated from more persistent income components (Hann et al. 2007).

To be sure, other factors such as competitive markets and rising costs from demographic aging may be more serious problems than accounting. However, what is evident is that global convergence toward fair value pension accounting has compounded problems for defined benefit pensions, magnifying problematic short-term risks that in the long term are potentially manageable, as long as the firm remains solvent. Accounting change is therefore another "layer" in the pension paradigm creating

---

[2] In terms of pension liabilities, a market-based approach is also followed. The rules stipulate that the discount rate used should be based on high quality corporate bonds, generally considered to be at least AA rated.

a "threshold effect" in a relatively long causal process of institutional transformation (cf. Hacker 2004). If fair value provides a homogenous and seemingly reliable picture of pension obligations for investors to use in valuations and investment decision-making, what might be positive for them (easily comparable data across firms) compounds other problems associated with defined benefit pension provision by eliminating corporate flexibility with respect to managing the liability over the long term. Indeed, the traditional view toward corporate pension accounting was designed to help firms spread pension costs over time. One could counter, however, that fair value forces firms to recognize the immediacy of growing pension costs and limits their ability to forego actions that ensure that obligations are covered. Whatever the case may be, few firms are willing to assume such long-term liabilities.

Veiled Convergence

United Kingdom

The "perfect storm" of low asset returns and low interest rates at the beginning of the twenty-first century was a shock to most defined benefit pension plan sponsors in the United Kingdom, as it dramatically reversed funding levels. The promises made to beneficiaries far outweighed the assets available to cover them. It did not help that many pension plans had had comfortable surpluses in the 1990s, which allowed many of them to take extended contribution holidays. Although financial markets improved in subsequent years, suggesting funding conditions would have improved, many final salary defined benefit pensions, which were already seeing a decline in coverage, were effectively left to wither and die in the storm's wake (Langley 2008). Indeed, a large number of firms either closed their schemes to new members or wound them up completely. Arguably, funding deficits were not the only culprit in driving pension curtailment, as funding problems had also occurred in the past. Rather, the introduction of new pension accounting standards that dictated the way in which these deficits would be reported on corporate balance sheets, and thus managed by the firm, was a significant factor.

On November 30, 2000, the U.K. Accounting Standards Board (ASB) introduced Financial Reporting Standard (FRS) 17, a mark-to-market pension accounting standard.[3] Although the U.K. ASB did not require full implementation until after 2003, it did require firms to report pension accounting information following FRS 17 in the footnotes of financial statements. In this case, implementation did not have to wait until after 2003: the information was available for those willing to look and therefore relevant to decision-making and corporate financing. One study, for example, suggests that the rapid collapse of final salary pensions in the 2000–2002 period is directly attributable to the shift in accounting from actuarial smoothing to fair value pension accounting methods, particularly among firms with large pension liabilities (Klumpes et al. 2007).

Figure 6.2, which shows the number of active members in open and closed private sector defined benefit and defined contribution schemes, indicates a marked decline in defined benefit membership following the bursting of the dot-com bubble in 2001. Membership in defined benefit schemes open to new members more than halved by 2005, decreasing from 4.1 million to just over 2 million members, suggesting that the appearance of new accounting standards was at least partially responsible for the rapid decline of defined benefit pension provision in the United Kingdom. By the end of the decade, membership in open private sector defined benefit schemes was a quarter of what it was at the beginning.

What is perhaps of more concern for retirement-income security in the United Kingdom is that the decline in occupational

[3] This standard is relatively consistent with IAS 19, which U.K. companies have had to follow since 2005

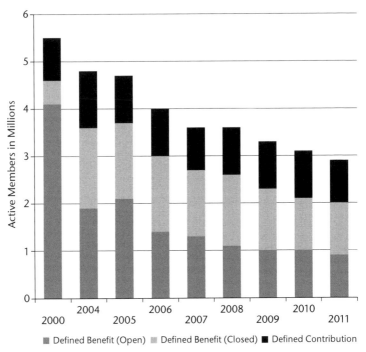

Figure 6.2 Occupational pension scheme coverage in the United Kingdom, 2000–2011

Source: Office for National Statistics, Occupational Pension Scheme Survey, 2011.

defined benefit pensions has not been met with subsequent replacement options in the occupational sphere. Whereas in the United States, for example, the decline of the defined benefit pension has been subsequently replaced on the whole by defined contribution schemes, U.K. employers have not responded to defined benefit closure with new defined contribution schemes. Indeed, in 1991 membership in defined contribution schemes in the United Kingdom accounted for roughly 900,000 workers. As of 2011, occupational defined contribution schemes still only account for 900,000 workers. Moreover, the total numbers of active members in employer-sponsored schemes decreased steadily from 6.5 million in 1991 to 2.9 million by 2011. Yet, this decline and resulting void is not the conclusion of occupational pensions in the United Kingdom. As we will discuss in the later subsection, Incoherence and Ambiguity, the U.K. government responded to the crisis of occupational pension coverage in 2008 by mandating that firms enroll employees in some type of pension scheme. Before doing so, we provide a contrast to the U.K. case by considering the transformation of defined benefit pensions in the Netherlands.

The Netherlands

Dutch occupational pension funds, with their internationally oriented investment strategies, were, like U.K. pension funds and sponsors, equally hit by the "perfect storm". In reaction, the Dutch pension regulator imposed strict funding requirements in 2002, which obligated pension funds to restore a liabilities coverage ratio of 105 percent by 2003. By law, then, Dutch pension funds had to quickly restore funding ratios, either by increasing contributions or altering the underlying pension contract. At the same time, Dutch pension funds, both corporate-sponsored and industry-wide, had to face the shift to fair value pension accounting due to the evolution of IFRS. These factors in combination led to a move away from the provision of final salary defined benefit pensions (Van Ewijk 2005). For instance, Akzo Nobel, a large chemical company, shifted its plan to a collective defined contribution scheme on July 1, 2005, with the CFO Rob Frohn noting that fluctuations in the market value of the pension plan were having a large effect on the firm's balance sheet. Similarly, SNS Reaal, a financial services firm, switched to a defined contribution plan on January 1, 2004. The trade union federation FNV noted that IFRS was the most important reason behind the pension alteration at SNS Reaal. Likewise, DSM, another large chemicals firm, switched to a defined contribution plan in June 2005. The new IFRS standards were a crucial component in the decision (Swinkels 2011).

However, in contrast to the United Kingdom and despite these examples, the response to new accounting standards and the shock of the "perfect storm" was different in the main. Instead of systematic closures, wind-ups, and thus increasing pension individualization, final salary defined benefit plans have shifted to an average salary formula, which determines the benefit based on the average wage over the total number of years worked—reducing some of the total cost in the process. Figure 6.3 displays this shift from final salary to average salary defined benefit, where a significant shift occurred between 2003 and 2004, or the period immediately before new accounting standards were to come into effect. In 2002 final salary defined benefit counted 3.2 million active members in 499 pension funds, or 54.3 percent of all workers with an occupational pension, whereas average salary counted 1.86 million active members in 182 pension funds, or 31.6 percent of workers. By 2007 only 183,000 active

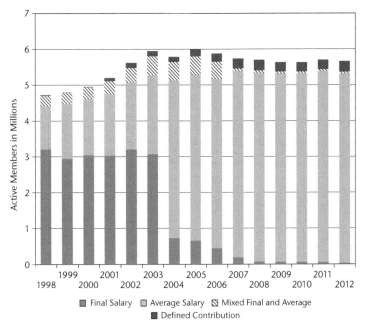

Figure 6.3 Occupational pension scheme coverage in the Netherlands, 1998–2012

Source: De Nederlandsche Bank

members in 84 pension funds still followed a final salary formula, whereas 5 million active members in 304 pension funds had converted to an average salary formula. The reform of the pension contract to average salary from 2004 at ABP and PGGM, the two largest pension funds, accounts for a large portion of the massive shift. At the same time, the growth of defined contribution pensions has been fairly limited, increasing from a negligible amount just before the millennium to nearly 300,000 active members by 2012, or roughly 5 percent of all active members in occupational pensions.

The real innovation for most Dutch pension plans during the period was the move to a solvency-contingent funding model, based on flexible indexation and flexible contributions. In periods of underfunding, when financial performance is poor and pension fund assets are inefficient to cover expected liabilities, the degree to which benefits keep up with an index (e.g. wage growth or inflation) may be reduced and/or contributions by current members increased. Benefits are still considered to follow a defined benefit method, because of how they are determined. In effect, these plans are neither defined benefit nor defined contribution, but rather a hybrid form where risks are shared among current members, retirees, and future participants. Note, however, that risk sharing occurs mainly among members of the plan; the long-term risk borne by the employer is ambiguous, as increased contributions occur through the wage contract and not through direct expenditure by the firm. Nevertheless, what is it specifically about the Dutch case insofar as firms are still partners in a modified form of the defined benefit pension, albeit one where firms have limited their long-term liabilities?

Mandated Solidarity

Moderated and pragmatic reform of Dutch occupational pensions—i.e. parametric reform rather than complete dissolution in the face of changing conditions—follows the institutional and statutory structure of the Dutch pension system in particular, and the institutionally embedded nature of Dutch social solidarity in general—an artifact not of recent origin but of significant historical depth. Not surprisingly, this implicit social solidarity has created a fairly coherent and rather flexible pension system in relative terms. To be sure, the Dutch pension system and pension funds are often trumpeted as a success story in comparison with other advanced economies, for the level of financial sophistication and embedded solidarity (see e.g. Ambachtsheer 2007; Haverland 2001).

There are four building blocks of social solidarity relevant to Dutch pensions policy (Clark 2003). In the first instance, near universal coverage of workers has been reached by means of indirect mandatory participation via collective contracts, which has been protected in statute since 1949 with the Law on Compulsory Participation in a Company Pension (Omtzigt 2007). Here, employers, employees, and social partners of a particular industry or business sector can devise an industry-wide pension fund, at which point all companies within the sector are obliged to participate. Non-participation is only allowed if a company has had a viable and comparable pension fund at least six months prior to the founding of the industry-wide scheme. In addition, employees are obliged to participate in an employer-offered fund, or when relevant, an industry-wide fund. As more than 90 percent of workers are members of either a company or industry-wide fund, this has made these "private" institutions ostensibly "public" in nature. This creates an active awareness of second-pillar pension schemes as crucial social institutions that are highly visible in Dutch society. As such, there is more resolve to sustain them for the long term even in the face of changing conditions.

In the second instance, there is equal representation of employers and employees on the boards of both corporate and industry-wide pension plans. As would be expected, the interests of both parties are taken into account, thus encouraging collective responsibility. Furthermore, board membership is often filled by those associated with sector-based collective bargaining. As such, structure and management of pension funds are permeated with the institutions and practices of Dutch collective bargaining. This follows into the third building block. For industry-wide plans, within which more than three-quarters of Dutch workers participate, pension benefits are set following compensation standards of the particular industry among firms and among workers. The solvency of the fund is therefore not dependent on the economic prospects of any single firm. Finally, the contribution levels to the fund are set at the industry level and through collective bargaining, which creates incentives to formulate the pension deal in a manner that would sustain long-term competitiveness of the industry, which in following helps assure the long-term solvency of the pension fund.

Despite this institutional structure of social solidarity, which by default "forces" firms as well as employees into a pension arrangement, there is still considerable support on both sides in the virtues and economic efficiency of collective provision and collective risk sharing. For those familiar with the Dutch political economy and its history, this follows the almost clichéd image of Dutch consensual corporatism and Dutch pragmatism in the face of new challenges and changing conditions (Kickert 2003). This is clearly demonstrated in the position of Dutch trade unions and employers' associations vis-à-vis occupational pension provision. As for trade unions, the 2003 collective bargaining round was deadlocked at many firms, due to efforts to renegotiate the pension contract. Initially the trade unions were fiercely opposed to many of these efforts, but eventually acquiesced to the need for rationalization around average salary, given the economic circumstances and new accounting standards. Moreover, as partially responsible for managing pension funds, the trade unions have been keen to see their continued sustainability in the face of changing demographic and economic conditions (Grünell 2003).

In February 2008, the major employers' organizations in the country (VNO-NCW, MKB-Nederland, LTO Nederland, and

Werkgeversvereniging AWVN) released a position paper outlining their commitment to a modern and affordable pension. The document argues that a good pension arrangement is part of the employment package of all employees now and in the future, and that solidarity and collective provision should be maintained, although with flexible boundaries following changing conditions, given this is historically embedded in Dutch labor relations. Significantly, the organizations note that despite their commitment, the Dutch second pillar faces a variety of threats, particularly excessive and inappropriate national and European legislation, and the shift to fair value accounting in IFRS.[4]

Incoherence and Ambiguity

Having documented how local institutional factors have impacted economic outcomes with respect to pension provision in the Netherlands, it is fruitful to return to the U.K. case to better understand how the political economy of pensions in the United Kingdom has led to a somewhat different but similar outcome. To be sure, occupational pensions in the United Kingdom have not had the strong institutional base seen in the Netherlands. Indeed, occupational pensions in general and final salary defined benefit pensions in particular have not been stable institutions in the U.K. pension system, especially in the private sector.

By some counts the United Kingdom has at least nine pensions systems in addition to the basic state pension. This has come as a result of pension policies that sought to solve problems or inefficiencies in the system by creating new sub-systems. Since 1946 the system has experienced major reforms at least once every decade. This has resulted in increasing complexity, policy incoherence, and ineffectiveness. This has led to

---

[4] VNO-NCW, MKB-NEDERLAND, LTO NEDERLAND and AWVN, 2008. *Naar een modern en betaalbaar pensioen: voorstellen voor een weerbaar en wendbaar pensioenstelsel* (Toward a modern and affordable pension: proposal for a strong and flexible pension system.).

lower coverage rates, scheme closure when difficult situations arise, or in the case of occupational provision, many employers not offering any pension schemes at all (Pemberton 2006). In terms of benefit design, final salary as a uniform practice existed for a relatively short period of time. Moreover, pension promises were not fixed and were often subject to significant alteration throughout the twentieth century. The landscape of benefit design and structure was actually quite diverse. Defined contribution-type "money purchase" and average salary were quite often the norm for many occupational schemes in the first half of the twentieth century. As Hannah (1986: 105) notes in his history of the development of U.K. occupational pensions, "pension schemes, when they were inaugurated, usually promised a level of retirement benefits in an apparently firm formula, which was felt at the time to suit the needs of employer and members alike;" however over the life of the scheme, "it was rare for the original benefit structure to have been retained."

Final salary defined benefit pensions did not become widely practiced until the late 1960s, reaching roughly two-thirds in the early 1970s. The increase in public sector employment and employment in state-owned firms in the immediate post-Second World War decades was crucial to this development. At the same time, the inadequacy of the state pension drove demand from employees for earnings-related pensions. This pushed employers to provide such benefits, which for them proved beneficial in terms of retaining employees during the tight labor market of the period. By 1979 roughly 92 percent of occupational pension schemes used a similar final salary formula based generally on the last year or last three years of employment (Hannah 1986: 105). As this indicates, final salary defined benefit pensions only came to prominence when membership in occupational pensions had already begun to decline after peaking in 1967. This reveals that final salary did not experience a long period of extensive growth and sustainability in the U.K. political economy, or occupational pensions in general for that matter. Final salary was short-lived at best. Moreover, given the relative paucity of coverage, gender and class inequalities in pension provision were perpetuated (Ginn and Arber 1991). Unlike in the Netherlands, then, where coverage spreads across most social strata, corporate-sponsored pensions never became strongly embedded as a social institution. Consequently, when accounting and regulatory changes made defined benefit a corporate burden, in comparison to the Netherlands, it was relatively easy to dismantle.

This fragility and unsettledness can also be explicated as a case of herd behavior within the "organizational field" of corporate sponsors.[5] For example, Bridgen and Meyer (2005) suggest that when large companies such as HSBC, Lloyds, and WH Smith closed their defined benefit schemes in the mid-1990s to new members—as their views changed vis-à-vis the cost-to-benefit ratio of defined benefit provision—this set the initial conditions for the wider disengagement within the organizational field. Against the backdrop of the "perfect storm", changes (or expected changes) in accounting rules, new longevity tables, and changes in government policy such as the 2004 Pensions Act,[6] knowledge of past successes by other very large firms established a benchmark of acceptability and facilitation. As Bridgen and Meyer (2005: 780) put it, "as knowledge became increasingly established in this way there was less and less need for individual actors to weigh up all options and their long-term consequences in order to make a decision. Instead, they were able to decide simply by referring to these ready-made options and by the thought that they were 'keeping up with the Joneses'." In addition to this, the layering of new pension sub-systems as suggested above—specifically the introduction of personal pensions in the 1986 Social Security Act as part of the Conservative Party's effort to promote individual property ownership and pension provision—arguably facilitated corporate disengagement from

---

[5] Organizational fields are sets of organizations that interact and consider each others' actions in their decision-making (see e.g. DiMaggio and Powell 1983).

[6] The 2004 Pensions Act solidified the burden for firms by establishing statutory funding requirements.

pension provision over time, as the supposed need for corporate involvement became less (Waine 1995).

But this is not the end of the narrative on occupational pension provision in the United Kingdom. The decline of the defined benefit pension and the solidarity it engendered between the firm and the work invokes an image of a triumphant neoliberalism. Overemphasizing neoliberalism, which is undoubtedly a powerful force in both explicit and implicit forms, runs the risk of overshadowing actual historical conditions and more importantly to emergent institutions. U.K. pension policy in the current era of individualization is increasingly being inculcated with mechanisms such as auto-enrollment, as a means of increasing retirement savings and overcoming high costs of individual decision-making. Individuals and firms have not been left completely to their own devices.

Responding to the rapid decline of defined benefit pensions and occupational pension provision more generally, the U.K. parliament, controlled then by the Labour Party, passed a new Pensions Act in 2008 that mandated employers to automatically enroll employees aged 22 and older in either an employer-sponsored pension scheme or the National Employment Savings Trust, which was also established by the Act. Rollout of what is effectively another layer in the U.K. pension system was set to occur between 2012 and 2018. In mandating occupational pension provision, the United Kingdom is actually moving closer to the Dutch model, where occupational pension provision has been enshrined in law since 1949. Differences still exist, particularly in institutional form, but there is increasing functional similarity.

Conclusions

In the context of a shareholder value paradigm, corporate decision-making revolves around maximization of market value on financial markets, rather than the more traditional production related questions of "what?", "where?", and "how much?".

As financial markets have become global, it is difficult for firms to be isolated from market expectations. As a result, national systems of economic organization and corporate governance are no longer protected and insulated from the influence of globally connected financial markets and their associated actors, and thus the possibility of being priced against competing opportunities. In seeking out investment capital and breaking the bonds of local financial systems, corporations subject themselves and their conduct to the conventional logic and expectations of the market.

A firm with defined benefit pension liabilities can run up against these expectations of financial institutions. If and when a firm is seen to be struggling with these obligations, which may suggest current and future cash flow diversions to redress a deficit, the firm risks engendering a negative reaction by investors; a simple discounted cash flow calculation may persuade investors of a negative effect on a firm's financial value. The more burdensome these pension commitments become, which fair value can magnify, the more costly they will be in terms of the discount ascribed by financial markets. In the long run, defined benefit plans may be seen as a risk best avoided, which would explain the general decline in the provision of defined benefit pensions globally.

There is one other systemic factor important to this narrative that deserves attention: the declining strength of trade unions. In the first instance, the apex and subsequent decline of defined benefit coverage is partially correlated to the density of trade union membership. In the 1960s union density averaged 40 percentage of total employment, increasing to 48 percent during the 1970s, and declining thereafter to less than 30 percent in the 2000s, as firms with low rates of unionization and pension plan coverage came to replace the declining and heavily-unionized manufacturing sector. Accordingly, a potential force mitigating the decline of occupational pension coverage was increasingly absent. This contrasts with the Netherlands where the social partners remain a key vector in the pension paradigm.

But even there, union density has decreased rapidly from 40 percent in 1960 to less than 20 percent by the mid-2000s.[7] Hence, although social solidarity is seemingly strong and healthy in the Netherlands, the recent transformation of defined benefit pensions can easily be read as a staging ground and source of legitimacy for further individualization of retirement-income security. The redesign of pension benefits has led to a redistribution of value to younger workers at the expense of older workers and retirees, whose shorter remaining lifetime limits their capacity to absorb risk, leading some to suggest that the "jury is still out" on the redesign's long-term trajectory (Ponds and van Riel 2009). Praising the virtues of Dutch social solidarity may be premature.

For some, the growing significance of financial markets in society foretells a degradation of institutional boundaries and historical solidarities in this search for higher and higher rates of return (Blackburn 2006). With the rise of finance and the homogenization and global spread of its associated practices and expectations—such as the harmonization of accounting standards—the forces working against spatial political–economic divergence are undoubtedly strong in the sphere of occupational pension provision. In both the United Kingdom and the Netherlands, accounting harmonization around the fair value method catalyzed ongoing processes of pension transformation and restructuring where the final salary defined benefit pension has become outmoded in the face of rising longevity and global competition. However, as the case of the Netherlands exhibits, historically contingent institutional settings are not broken down that easily. The emergence of new challenges both internally and externally elicits a recombination and bricolage of existing institutional structures, habits, and cultural-cognitive conventions.

What is clear is that, on the one hand, the rise of finance and what it brings along with it (forces of homogenization) needs

[7] See OECD Database on Trade Unions.

to be taken seriously as a source of change that cuts across borders. On the other hand, analytical care must be exercised as to the degree of power and spatial influence given to finance and its capacity to drive convergence. Political economies remain institutionally distinct in some ways regardless of increasing amounts of financialization. Convergence and homogenization are occurring and will undoubtedly continue to occur. Nevertheless, discernable formal differences may persist as well. Although firms may defect from the traditions of coordination present in the political economy, this does not mean that social solidarity is necessarily eroded. The continued salience of social solidarity in many advanced European democracies, e.g. Sweden and the Netherlands, partially masks the many forms of liberalization underway. In this manner, convergence is not necessarily total, but rather veiled. Convergence is veiled in the sense that political economies and firm behavior may show increasingly common trends, but other policies and cultural traits may continue to fill the void of the previously coordinated institutional environment, thus masking significant institutional change elsewhere.

7

The Global Financial Crisis and Beyond

For a book concerned in part with the place of finance in the changing geography of capitalism, some may wonder why the most recent global financial crisis does not figure more centrally in the text. Indeed, the global financial crisis has put in stark relief a world economy punctuated clearly by winners and losers. For emerging economies, particularly in East Asia, the global financial crisis was a mere blip on an upward growth trajectory that seems far from subsiding. In other parts of the world, particularly in the peripheries of Europe, the financial crisis has put into question the sustainability of state commitments to the welfare of its citizens in the face of anemic growth. The long-term prospects of entire regions are in doubt. If some thought that the global financial crisis would result in a taming of the power of finance and our collective reliance on the performance of markets, it is unclear if much has actually changed. One reason for not centering the narrative around the global financial crisis, notwithstanding the increasingly crowded field of academic and popular contributions, is that the arguments and implications of this book precede and transcend the global financial crisis. Nonetheless, some of its curious non-outcomes provide a useful starting point on which to conclude our discussion.

When the 2007–2008 subprime financial crisis transitioned into a sovereign debt crisis in Europe, it was not uncommon to hear arguments in the popular media about a pending breakup of the Eurozone, reinforced by active calls for some countries to be ejected and for others to join together in a new European monetary union. The standard logic of the arguments was that the Eurozone was an impediment to restoring growth and resetting the terms of trade of member countries on a more sustainable footing. Indeed, for countries on the periphery, namely Greece, having the euro has made it impossible to adjust its trade competitiveness through depreciation of the currency—an external devaluation. A restoration of competitiveness—or rather a downward adjustment of prices and wages below that of its trading partners—would have to come through an internal devaluation driven by slow or negative growth. Anemic domestic demand and high unemployment serve to push prices and wages down. But an internal devaluation is a difficult and painful socioeconomic process. It is furthermore painful when coupled with harsh government austerity and reform of the public sector, as the Greek government tries to achieve the terms of the IMF-led bailout loan that is meant to prevent a sovereign default. With Greek GDP having declined by more than 25 percent between 2008 and 2012, and growth seemingly without reach, it is curious that Greece has not exited the Eurozone. Would not an external devaluation set Greece on a more rapid path to recovery, as proponents of an exit argue?

To be sure, the global financial crisis has resulted in an existential crisis for the Eurozone that is not yet settled. For what was a project aimed at driving economic growth and development through market expansion and integration—which it undoubtedly did prior to the crisis—it did not prevent the clear and dramatic appearance of regional winners and losers that puts the entire European project in doubt. But is the existence of the Eurozone, or for that matter the European Union, really in doubt? After more than five years of difficult economic conditions for many citizens in the Eurozone, why has the Eurozone persisted? Why have we not seen a return to national currencies and thus clearly defined national economies? If one is to take seriously the argument of this book, one explanation for this is that the geography of capitalism has fundamentally changed. National economies are more interconnected and interdependent. What would a return to clearly defined national economies look like? How are these interconnections and interdependencies that transcend national economic space unwound? If firms are central to economic growth and development, and therefore any national production system, how can firms be re-embedded in support of the national economy? How are firms that have been unshackled from their history and geography by the globalization of supply chains and the globalization of finance be re-shackled and re-identified as a national economic concern?

For decades firms have been constructing increasingly complex and extensive supply chains through outsourcing and offshoring, making investments and building capacity across countries. In the Eurozone, these investments were made under the assumption that monetary union would persist. Reconfiguring these transnational networks and their territorial scope is not impossible, but it would be costly and disruptive. Moreover, even if reconfiguration and re-territorialization is possible, it does not follow necessarily that such renewal will entail any sort of durable renationalization of production.[1] One can assume that governments and firms alike at the core of the Eurozone are aware of this, even if they may not readily acknowledge it. It may be clichéd to say that the national interest is what is good for business both at home and abroad, but governments at the core of Europe, Germany in particular, have put their credit rating on the line in keeping the Eurozone intact; they have seemed unwilling to risk collapse for fear of the social and economic costs it may bring. Governments at the core are furthermore concerned about having to bail out the

---

[1] Note that the use of the term renationalization here does not mean a return to state ownership. Renationalization here means the re-emergence of a clearly definable national production system.

banks and other institutional investors that are under their prudential supervision and lent capital to the periphery.

If the actions of governments in the Eurozone to keep the monetary union intact appear to be about protecting the interests of national firms, this is not necessarily the correct assumption. One interpretation for governments' willingness to hold the system together is that individually and collectively they are not certain of the loyalties of firms, even if some notional evidence (e.g. corporate headquarters) of a firm's national identity can be grasped. If the arguments in this book are to be taken seriously, then one can assume that governments are well aware of the options and incentives available to firms—which governments have facilitated since the end of the Second World War—by way of global financial markets and outsourcing and offshoring. If firms are unwilling to assume the long-term welfare of the average worker, as Chapter 6 argued, then what evidence exists that firms are committed to any particular national economy? Moreover, what is their concern for the national economy, if their ownership is dispersed across investors from around the world and their financial needs are met, furthermore, by capital markets that are global in reach? Indeed, as argued in Chapters 1 and 4, the borders of national financial systems have become increasingly porous, complicating efforts to locate the extent of the borders of financial systems and thus the incentives facing firms. But even if borders can be found, policy convergence, practice convergence, and financial innovation, have eroded formal differences. How, then, are financial systems *national* financial systems?

At this point some readers may question this argument as being hyperbolic—equivalent to the hyper-globalization theses of the popular variety. If a somewhat accurate reading, the implied hyperbole serves to emphasize the significance of global economic change in the twenty-first century. Those that downplay globalization, if for want of a former Golden Age of capitalism, are missing fundamental changes that have unleashed capital from the shackles of history and geography. But the argument offered in this book, particularly in Chapters 2 and 3, is still one that sees a crucial role for place and institutional diversity. Recall that the global mosaic of regional economies is one marked by Ricardian–Listian competition, where regions find competitive advantage through institutionally-mediated locational specialization. These large megalopolitan city regions with their multifaceted local labor markets, intricate networks of specialized but complementary forms of economic activity, drive the global economy. Globalization does not erode the power of place, it reinforces it.

But just because place matters, that does not mean the unique institutional features of a place should be held constant and impervious to change. And just because some institutional features are unique formally, it does not mean that another place with ostensibly different formal institutional features cannot produce the same outcomes. As argued in Chapters 1 and 3, the form of an institution does not necessarily determine its function, and institutional function does not necessarily determine its form. Different institutional forms can produce analogous outcomes. A group of institutional investors acting in the space of the market, as highlighted in Chapter 4, can provide a firm with patient capital in the same fashion as a bank can. By breaking the causal assumption that form determines function or that function determines form, we can better appreciate variable rates of change in either. National (and regional) economies can be institutionally distinct in terms of form in any number of ways. Occupational pensions in the Netherlands, for example, have more entrenched solidarity than in the United Kingdom, suggesting a different institutional form, but firms in both places have unburdened themselves from the responsibility of guaranteeing a lifelong income. Formal differences may persist, but under the surface major changes are underway. Recognizing and appreciating the significance of these underlying changes is important, as they put into question the long-term stability of those formal institutional features that appear unchanged.

Some readers may find it paradoxical that a warning is given in the initial chapters of the book on the problems with methodological nationalism, only to be followed subsequently by empirical chapters that deal with issues through the lens of the national scale. However, a warning against methodological nationalism does not mean that the national scale ceases to be relevant as an analytical category or as a crucial site of economic governance. Again, globalization does not erode the power of place, it reinforces it. The basic premise of the warning against methodological nationalism is that systematically privileging one scale over another risks obfuscating the significance of space spanning networks of economic activity that transcend national borders, or institutional variability at the sub-national scale, for understanding national political economies under conditions of global economic integration and increasing extraterritorial interdependence.

It is this frame of reference that, for instance, underwrites the analysis of the changing welfare state in Chapter 5. The example of France and its new pension reserve fund demonstrates the increasing integration of financial logics at the heart of the pension system, as recognition that achieving adequate retirement security rests on capturing the value generated from the global economy through investing in global financial markets. National systems of social protection are increasingly financialized. But financialization does not necessarily entail a triumph of neoliberalism. It is true that individuals are increasingly responsible for a greater proportion of their long-term income security. But governments are not simply leaving the fate of individuals to their own devices. For example, the United Kingdom, as noted in Chapter 6, has mandated pension savings, while coordinating a government-sponsored institutional investor in the form of the National Employment Savings Trust to assist in that regard.

It is tempting to end on a speculative note looking out into the future. But doing so is not so straightforward. The historical geography of capitalism is one of change. Holding history and geography constant, assuming that institutional forms and functions are comfortably embedded and unmovable, discounts capitalism's inherent drive to innovate and expand markets. It is clear, nonetheless, that global financial markets and global supply chains will continue to be a prominent feature of the geography of capitalism from the global to the local, providing firms with new and different incentives, while driving institutional change across different political economies. This does not mean that diversity of the economic landscape will disappear. Yet, diversity should not be overstated. If there is value in understanding diversity, it is of equal value that we understand what is the same about different capitalist economies and how interconnected and interdependent they have become.

References

Agnew, J. 1994. The territorial trap: the geographical assumptions of international relations theory. *Review of International Political Economy* 1:53–80.

Alber, J. 1981. Government responses to the challenge of unemployment: the development of unemployment insurance in Western Europe. In *The development of welfare states in Europe and America*, ed. P. Flora and A. Heidenheimer, 151–183. New Brunswick, NJ; London: Transaction.

Albert, M. 1991. *Capitalisme contre capitalisme*. Paris: Seuil.

Aldcroft, D.H. 2001. *The European economy, 1914–2000*. London: Routledge.

Allen, F. and D. Gale. 2000. *Comparing financial systems*. Cambridge, MA; London: MIT Press.

Amable, B. 2003. *The diversity of modern capitalism*. Oxford: Oxford University Press.

Ambachtsheer, K.P. 2007. *Pension revolution: a solution to the pensions crisis*. Hoboken, NJ: John Wiley & Sons.

Amin, A. 2002. Spatialities of globalisation. *Environment and Planning A* 34:385–399.

Amin, A. 2004. Regions unbound: towards a new politics of place. *Geografiska Annaler: Series B, Human Geography* 86:33–44.

Amin, A. (ed.). 1994. *Post-Fordism: a reader*. Oxford: Blackwell.

Amin, A. and N.J. Thrift. (eds). 1994. Globalization, institutions, and regional development in Europe. Oxford; New York: Oxford University Press.

Amin, S. 1973. *Le développement inégal*. Paris: Minuit.

Arrighi, G. 1994. *The long twentieth century: money, power and the origins of our times*. London: Verso.

Auerbach, A., L. Kotlikoff, and W. Leibfritz. 1999. *Generational accounting around the world*. Chicago, IL: University of Chicago Press.

Baldwin, P. 1990. *The politics of social solidarity: class bases of the European welfare state: 1875–1975*. Cambridge: Cambridge University Press.

Barker, R.M. 2010. *Corporate governance, competition, and political parties: explaining corporate governance change in Europe.* Oxford: Oxford University Press.

Barr, M. 2005. Credit where it counts: the Community Reinvestment Act and its critics. *New York University Law Review* 75:117–233.

Barr, N.A. 2001. *The welfare state as piggy bank: information, risk, uncertainty, and the role of the state.* Oxford: Oxford University Press.

Bathelt, H. and M.S. Gertler. 2005. The German variety of capitalism: forces and dynamics of evolutionary change. *Economic Geography* 81:1–9.

Bathelt, H. and J. Glückler. 2003. Toward a relational economic geography. *Journal of Economic Geography* 3:117–144.

Bathelt, H. and J. Glückler. 2011. *The relational economy: geographies of knowing and learning.* Oxford: Oxford University Press.

Bauer, R., R. Braun, and G.L. Clark. 2008. The emerging market for European corporate governance: the relationship between governance and capital expenditures, 1997–2005. *Journal of Economic Geography* 8:441–469.

Beck, T., A. Demirgüç-Kunt, and V. Maksimovic. 2008. Financing patterns around the world: are small firms different? *Journal of Financial Economics* 89:467–487.

Benston, G. 2006. Fair-value accounting: a cautionary tale from Enron. *Journal of Accounting and Public Policy* 25:465–484.

Berger, A.N. and G.F. Udell. 2002. Small business credit availability and relationship lending: the importance of bank organisational structure. *The Economic Journal* 112:F32–F53.

Berger, A.N. and G.F. Udell. 2006. A more complete conceptual framework for SME finance. *Journal of Banking & Finance* 30:2945–2966.

Berger, A.N., R.J. Rosen, and G.F. Udell. 2007. Does market size structure affect competition? The case of small business lending. *Journal of Banking & Finance* 31:11–33.

Berger, S. and R. Dore (eds). 1996. *National diversity and global capitalism.* Ithaca, NY; London: Cornell University Press.

Beyer, J. 2003. Deutschland AG a.D: Deutsche Bank, Allianz und das Verflechtungszentrum des deutschen Kapitalismus. In *Alle Macht dem Markt? Fallstudien zur Abwicklung der Deutschland AG*, ed. W. Streeck and M. Höpner, 118–146. Frankfurt: Campus Verlag.

Bignon, V., Y. Biondi, and X. Ragot. 2004. An economic analysis of fair value: the evolution of accounting principles in European legislation, with a commentary by R.G. Barker (Cambridge University and IASB Scientific Committee) and a rejoinder by the authors. *Prisme* 4:22–25.

Biondi, Y. and T. Suzuki. 2007. Socio-economic impacts of international accounting standards: an introduction. *Socio-Economic Review* 5:585–602.

Blackburn, R. 2002. *Banking on death: or, investing in life: the history and future of pensions.* London: Verso.

Blackburn, R. 2006. *Age shock: how finance is failing us.* London; New York: Verso.

Bluestone, B. and B. Harrison. 1982. *The deindustrialization of America: plant closings, community abandonment, and the dismantling of basic industry.* New York: Basic Books.

Bluhm, K. and B. Martens. 2009. Recomposed institutions: smaller firms' strategies, shareholder-value orientation and bank relationships in Germany. *Socio-Economic Review* 7:585–604.

Blyth, M. 2003. Same as it never was: temporality and typology in the varieties of capitalism. *Comparative European Politics* 1:215–225.

Boschma, R.A. and K. Frenken. 2006. Why is economic geography not an evolutionary science? Towards an evolutionary economic geography. *Journal of Economic Geography* 6:273–302.

Boschma, R. and R. Martin (eds). 2010. *The handbook of evolutionary economic geography.* Cheltenham: Edward Elgar.

Boyer, R. 2007. Assessing the impact of fair value upon financial crises. *Socio-Economic Review* 5:779–807.

Braudel, F. 1984. *Civilization and capitalism. Vol. 3: The perspective of the world.* London: W. Collins.

Brenner, N. 2004. *New state spaces: urban governance and the rescaling of statehood.* Oxford: Oxford University Press.

Brenner, N. (ed.). 2003. *State/space: a reader.* Malden, MA; Oxford: Blackwell.

Brenner, N., J. Peck, and N. Theodore. 2010. Variegated neoliberalization: geographies, modalities, pathways. *Global Networks* 10:182–222.

Bridgen, P. and T. Meyer. 2005. When do benevolent capitalists change their mind? Explaining the retrenchment of defined-benefit pensions in Britain. *Social Policy & Administration* 39:764–785.

Briggs, A. 1961. The welfare state in historical perspective. *European Journal of Sociology/Archives Européennes de Sociologie* 2:221–258.

Brinson, G., B. Singer, and G. Beebower. 1991. Determinants of portfolio performance II: an update. *Financial Analysts Journal* 47:40–48.

Brunner, A., J. Decressin, D. Hardy, and B. Kudela. 2004. *Germany's three-pillar banking system: cross-country perspectives in Europe, Occasional Paper.* Washington, DC: International Monetary Fund (IMF).

Bryson, J.R., P.W. Daniels, and B. Warf. 2004. *Service worlds: people, organisations, technologies*. London: Routledge.

Burger, C. 2012. Geography of savings in the German occupational pension system. *Regional Studies* Published online 18 Jul 2012.

Busemeyer, M. and C. Trampusch (eds). 2012. The political economy of collective skill formation. Oxford: Oxford University Press.

Bushee, B. 2004. Identifying and attracting the "right" investors: evidence on the behavior of institutional investors. *Journal of Applied Corporate Finance* 16:28–35.

Cairncross, F. 1997. *The death of distance: how the communications revolution will change our lives*. Boston, MA: Harvard Business School Press.

Campbell, J.Y. and L.M. Viceira. 2002. *Strategic asset allocation: portfolio choice for long-term investors*. New York: Oxford University Press.

Castells, M. 1996. *The rise of the network society*. Cambridge, MA; Oxford: Blackwell.

Castles, F. 2004. *The future of the welfare state: crisis myths and crisis realities*. Oxford: Oxford University Press.

Christophers, B. 2013. *Banking across boundaries: placing finance in capitalism*. Oxford: Wiley-Blackwell.

Christopherson, S. 2002. Why do national labor market practices continue to diverge in the global economy? The "missing link" of investment rules. *Economic Geography* 78:1–20.

Christopherson, S., J. Michie, and P. Tyler. 2010. Regional resilience: theoretical and empirical perspectives. *Cambridge Journal of Regions, Economy and Society* 3:3–10.

Cioffi, J.W. 2002. Restructuring "Germany Inc.": the politics of company and takeover law reform in Germany and the European Union. *Law & Policy* 24:355–402.

Clark, G.L. 2000. *Pension fund capitalism*. Oxford: Oxford University Press.

Clark, G.L. 2003. *European pensions & global finance*. Oxford: Oxford University Press.

Clark, G.L. and D. Wójcik. 2007. *The geography of finance: corporate governance in the global marketplace*. Oxford: Oxford University Press.

Clark, G.L., A.D. Dixon, and A.H.B. Monk. 2013. *Sovereign wealth funds: legitimacy, governance, and global power*. Princeton, NJ; Oxford: Princeton University Press.

Clark, G.L. and N. Wrigley. 1997a. Exit, the firm and sunk costs: reconceptualizing the corporate geography of disinvestment and plant closure. *Progress in Human Geography* 21:338–358.

Clark, G.L. and N. Wrigley. 1997b. The spatial configuration of the firm and the management of sunk costs. *Economic Geography* 73:285–304.

Clark, G.L., A.D. Dixon, and A.H.B. Monk. (eds). 2009. *Managing financial risks: from global to local*. Oxford: Oxford University Press.

Clift, B. 2006. The new political economy of dirigisme: French macroeconomic policy, unrepentant sinning and the Stability and Growth Pact. *British Journal of Politics and International Relations* 8:388–409.

Clowes, M.J. 2000. *The money flood: how pension funds revolutionized investing*. New York: Wiley.

Coase, R. 1937. The nature of the firm. *Economica* 4:386–405.

Coe, N., P. Dicken, and M. Hess. 2008. Global production networks: realizing the potential. *Journal of Economic Geography* 8:271–295.

Cole, R.A. 2008. What do we know about the capital structure of privately held firms? Evidence from the Surveys of Small Business Finance. *SSRN eLibrary*.

Cole, R.A., L.G. Goldberg, and L.J. White. 2004. Cookie cutter vs. character: the micro structure of small business lending by large and small banks. *Journal of Financial and Quantitative Analysis* 39:227–251.

Cooke, P. and K. Morgan. 1998. *The associational economy: firms, regions, and innovation*. Oxford: Oxford University Press.

Corbett, J. and T. Jenkinson. 1996. The financing of industry, 1970–1989: an international comparison. *Journal of the Japanese and International Economies* 10:71–96.

Corbett, J. and T. Jenkinson. 1997. How is investment financed? A study of Germany, Japan, the United Kingdom and the United States. *The Manchester School* 65:69–93.

Craig, B., W. Jackson, and J. Thomson. 2008. Credit market failure intervention: do government sponsored small business credit programs enrich poorer areas? *Small Business Economics* 30:345–360.

Crane, D., K. Froot, S. Mason, A. Perold, R. Merton, Z. Bodie, E. Sirri, and P. Tufano. 1995. *The global financial system: a functional perspective*. Boston, MA: Harvard Business School Press.

Critchfield, T.S., K. Samolyk, L. Davison, G. Hanc, H. Gratton, and T. Davis. 2004. Future of banking in America—community banks: their recent past, current performance, and future prospects. *FDIC Banking Review* 16:1–55.

Crouch, C. 2005. *Capitalist diversity and change: recombinant governance and institutional entrepreneurs*. Oxford: Oxford University Press.

Culpepper, P. 2005. Institutional change in contemporary capitalism: coordinated financial systems since 1990. *World Politics* 57:173–199.

Davis, E.P. and B. Steil. 2001. *Institutional investors*. Cambridge, MA; London: MIT.

De Bonis, R., D. Fano, and T. Sbano. 2013. Household aggregate wealth in the main OECD countries from 1980 to 2011: what do the data tell us? *Questioni di Economia e Finanza (Occasional Papers, 160)*, Rome: Banca D'Italia, Economic Research and International Relations Area.

Deeg, R. 1999. *Finance capitalism unveiled: banks and the German political economy*. Ann Arbor, MI: University of Michigan Press.

Deeg, R. 2009. The rise of internal capitalist diversity? Changing patterns of finance and corporate governance in Europe. *Economy and Society* 38:552–579.

Deeg, R. and G. Jackson. 2007. Towards a more dynamic theory of capitalist variety. *Socio-Economic Review* 5:149–179.

DeYoung, R. 2007. Safety, soundness, and the evolution of the U.S. banking industry. *Economic Review*:41–66.

DeYoung, R., W.C. Hunter, and G.F. Udell. 2004. The past, present, and probable future for community banks. *Journal of Financial Services Research* 25:85–133.

Diamond, D.W. 1984. Financial intermediation and delegated monitoring. *Review of Economic Studies* 51:393–414.

Dicken, P. and A. Malmberg. 2001. Firms in territories: a relational perspective. *Economic Geography* 77:345–363.

Dicken, P. and N. Thrift. 1992. The organization of production and the production of organization: why business enterprises matter in the study of geographical industrialization. *Transactions of the Institute of British Geographers* 17:279–291.

DiMaggio, P.J., and W.W. Powell. 1983. The iron cage revisited: institutional isomorphism and collective rationality in organizational fields. *American Sociological Review* 48:147–160.

Dimson, E., P. Marsh, and M. Staunton. 2002. *Triumph of the optimists: 101 years of global investment returns*. Princeton, NJ; Oxford: Princeton University Press.

Dittmann, I., E. Maug, and C. Schneider. 2010. Bankers on the boards of German firms: what they do, what they are worth, and why they are (still) there. *Review of Finance* 14:35–71.

Dixon, A.D. 2009. Finding the collective in an era of pension individualization. *Soziale Welt* 60:47–62.

Dixon, A.D. 2011. Variegated capitalism and the geography of finance: towards a common agenda. *Progress in Human Geography* 35:193–210.

Dixon, A.D. 2012. Function before form: macro-institutional comparison and the geography of finance. *Journal of Economic Geography* 12:579–600.

Dixon, A.D. and A.H.B. Monk. 2009. The power of finance: accounting harmonization's effect on pension provision. *Journal of Economic Geography* 9:619–639.

Dixon, A.D. and V. Sorsa. 2009. Institutional change and the financialisation of pensions in Europe. *Competition & Change* 13:347–367.

Djelic, M.-L. and S. Quack. 2007. Overcoming path dependency: path generation in open systems. *Theory and Society* 36:161–186.

Djelic, M.-L. and S. Quack. 2010. *Transnational communities: shaping global economic governance.* Cambridge: Cambridge University Press.

Doellgast, V. and I. Greer. 2007. Vertical disintegration and the disorganization of German industrial relations. *British Journal of Industrial Relations* 45:55–76.

Dooley, M., D. Folkerts-Landau, and P. Garber. 2004. The revived Bretton Woods system. *International Journal of Finance & Economics* 9:307–313.

Dore, R. 2008. Financialization of the global economy. *Industrial and Corporate Change* 17:1097–1112.

Drucker, P.F. 1976. *The unseen revolution: how pension fund socialism came to America.* New York: Harper & Row.

Drucker, S. and M. Puri. 2005. On the benefits of concurrent lending and underwriting. *Journal of Finance* 60:2763–2799.

Dunning, J.H. 1993. *The globalization of business: the challenge of the 1990s.* London: Routledge.

Dupuy, C., S. Lavigne, and D. Nicet-Chenaf. 2010. Does geography still matter? Evidence on the portfolio turnover of large equity investors and varieties of capitalism. *Economic Geography* 86:75–98.

Dymski, G.A. 2009. The global financial customer and the spatiality of exclusion after the 'end of geography'. *Cambridge Journal of Regions, Economy and Society* 2:267–285.

Ebbinghaus, B. (ed.). 2011. *The varieties of pension governance: pension privatization in Europe.* Oxford: Oxford University Press.

Edwards, J. and K. Fischer. 1994. *Banks, finance and investment in Germany.* Cambridge: Cambridge University Press.

Eichengreen, B. 2008. *Globalizing capital: a history of the international monetary system.* Princeton, NJ: Princeton University Press.

Eichengreen, B. 2011. *Exorbitant privilege: the rise and fall of the dollar.* Oxford: Oxford University Press.

Elsas, R. 2005. Empirical determinants of relationship lending. *Journal of Financial Intermediation* 14:32–57.

Elyasiani, E. and L.G. Goldberg. 2004. Relationship lending: a survey of the literature. *Journal of Economics and Business* 56:315–330.

Engel, D. and T. Middendorf. 2009. Investment, internal funds and public banking in Germany. *Journal of Banking & Finance* 33:2132–2139.

Engelen, E. 2006. Changing work patterns and the reorganization of occupational pensions. In *Oxford handbook of pensions and retirement income*, ed. G.L. Clark, A.H. Munnell, and M. Orszag, 98–116. Oxford: Oxford University Press.

Engelen, E. and J. Faulconbridge. 2009. Introduction: financial geographies—the credit crisis as an opportunity to catch economic geography's next boat? *Journal of Economic Geography* 9:587–595.

Engelen, E. and M. Grote. 2009. Stock exchange virtualisation and the decline of second-tier financial centres—the cases of Amsterdam and Frankfurt. *Journal of Economic Geography* 9:679–696.

Engelen, E., M. Konings, and R. Fernandez. 2010. Geographies of financialization in disarray: the Dutch case in comparative perspective. *Economic Geography* 86:53–73.

Engelen, E., I. Ertürk, J. Froud, J. Sukhdev, A. Leaver, M. Moran, A. Nilsson, and K. Williams. 2011. *After the great complacence: financial crisis and the politics of reform*. Oxford: Oxford University Press.

Esping-Andersen, G. 1990. *The three worlds of welfare capitalism*. Cambridge: Polity.

Fama, E. and K. French. 2002. The equity premium. *Journal of Finance* 57:637–659.

Farole, T., A. Rodríguez-Pose, and M. Storper. 2011. Human geography and the institutions that underlie economic growth. *Progress in Human Geography* 35:58–80.

Faulconbridge, J.R. 2004. London and Frankfurt in Europe's evolving financial centre network. *Area* 36:235–244.

Faulconbridge, J.R., E. Engelen, M. Hoyler, and J. Beaverstock. 2007. Analysing the changing landscape of European financial centres: the role of financial products and the case of Amsterdam. *Growth and Change* 38:279–303.

Feldman, M. 1994. *The geography of innovation*. Dordrecht; London: Kluwer Academic.

Ferrera, M. 2005. *The boundaries of welfare: European integration and the new spatial politics of social protection*. Oxford: Oxford University Press.

Florida, R. 1995. Toward the learning region. *Futures* 27:527–536.

Florida, R. and M. Kenney. 1988. Venture capital, high technology and regional development. *Regional Studies* 22:33–48.

Florida, R. and D. Smith. 1993. Venture capital formation, investment, and regional industrialization. *Annals of the Association of American Geographers* 83:434–451.

Franks, J. and C. Mayer. 2001. Ownership and control of German corporations. *Review of Financial Studies* 14:943–977.

French, K. and J. Poterba. 1991. Investor diversification and international equity markets. *American Economic Review* 81:222–226.

Friedman, T. 2006. *The world is flat: the globalized world in the twenty-first century.* London: Penguin.

Froud, J., S. Johal, A. Leaver, and K. Williams. 2006. *Financialization and strategy: narrative and numbers.* London: Routledge.

Froud, J., A. Leaver, and K. Williams. 2007. New actors in a financialised economy and the remaking of capitalism. *New Political Economy* 12:339–347.

Fröbel, F., J. Heinrichs, and O. Kreye. 1980. *The new international division of labour: structural unemployment in industrial countries and industrialisation in developing countries.* Cambridge: Cambridge University Press.

Fujita, M., P. Krugman, and A. Venables. 1999. *The spatial economy: cities, regions and international trade.* Cambridge, MA; London: MIT Press.

Fukuyama, F. 1992. *The end of history and the last man.* London: Penguin.

Garretsen, H., M. Kitson, and R. Martin. 2009. Spatial circuits of global finance. *Cambridge Journal of Regions, Economy and Society* 2:143–148.

George, V., P. Taylor-Gooby, and G. Bonoli. 2000. *European welfare futures: towards a theory of retrenchment.* Cambridge: Polity Press.

Gerschenkron, A. 1962. *Economic backwardness in historical perspective, a book of essays.* Cambridge, MA: Belknap Press of Harvard University Press.

Gertler, M.S. 1995. "Being there": proximity, organization, and culture in the development and adoption of advanced manufacturing technologies. *Economic Geography* 71:1–26.

Gertler, M.S. 2004. *Manufacturing culture: the institutional geography of industrial practice.* Oxford: Oxford University Press.

Gertler, M.S. 2010. Rules of the game: the place of institutions in regional economic change. *Regional Studies* 44:1–15.

Ghilarducci, T. 1992. *Labor's capital: the economics and politics of private pensions.* Cambridge, MA; London: MIT Press.

Ginn, J. and S. Arber. 1991. Gender, class and income inequalities in later life. *British Journal of Sociology* 42:369–396.

Glyn, A. 2006. *Capitalism unleashed: finance, globalization, and welfare.* Oxford; New York: Oxford University Press.

Goyer, M. 2011. *Contingent capital: short-term investors and the evolution of corporate governance in France and Germany.* Oxford: Oxford University Press.

Grabher, G. 1993. *The embedded firm: on the socioeconomics of industrial networks*. London, Routledge.

Gratton, H. 2004. Regional and other midsize banks: recent trends and short-term prospects. In *FDIC Future of Banking Study*. Washington, DC: FDIC.

Grossman, E. 2006. Europeanization as an interactive process: German public banks meet EU state aid policy. *Journal of Common Market Studies* 44:325–348.

Grossman, E. and P. Leblond. 2011. European financial integration: finally the great leap forward? *Journal of Common Market Studies* 49:413–435.

Grossman, G. and E. Helpman. 2005. Outsourcing in a global economy. *Review of Economic Studies* 72:135–159.

Grossman, G. and E. Rossi-Hansberg. 2008. Trading tasks: a simple theory of offshoring. *American Economic Review* 98:1978–1997.

Grünell, M. 2003. Deadlock on occupational pensions in company bargaining. *European Industrial Relations Observatory On-line*.

Grunson, M. and U. Schneider. 1995. The German Landesbanken. *Columbia Business Law Review* 1995:337–452.

Hacker, J.S. 2004. Privatizing risk without privatizing the welfare state: the hidden politics of social policy retrenchment in the United States. *American Political Science Review* 98:243–260.

Hackethal, A. 2004. German banks and banking structure. In *The German Financial System*, ed. J.P. Krahnen and R.H. Schmidt, 71–105. Oxford: Oxford University Press.

Hall, P.A. and D. Soskice (eds). 2001. *Varieties of capitalism: the institutional foundations of comparative advantage*. Oxford: Oxford University Press.

Hall, P.A. and K. Thelen. 2009. Institutional change in varieties of capitalism. *Socio-Economic Review* 7:7–34.

Hall, S. 2008. Geographies of business education: MBA programmes, reflexive business schools and the cultural circuit of capital. *Transactions of the Institute of British Geographers* 33:27–41.

Hall, S. 2011. Educational ties, social capital and the translocal (re)production of MBA alumni networks. *Global Networks* 11:118–138.

Hancké, B., M. Rhodes, and M. Thatcher (eds). 2007. *Beyond varieties of capitalism: conflict, contradictions, and complementarities in the European economy*. Oxford: Oxford University Press.

Hann, R.N., F. Heflin, and K.R. Subramanayam. 2007. Fair-value pension accounting. *Journal of Accounting and Economics* 44:328–358.

Hannah, L. 1986. *Inventing retirement: the development of occupational pensions in Britain*. Cambridge: Cambridge University Press.

Harhoff, D. and T. Körting. 1998. Lending relationships in Germany—empirical evidence from survey data. *Journal of Banking & Finance* 22:1317–1353.

Harmes, A. 1998. Institutional investors and the reproduction of neoliberalism. *Review of International Political Economy* 5:92–121.

Harris, J. 1997. *William Beveridge: a biography*. Oxford: Clarendon Press.

Harvey, D. 1982. *The limits to capital*. Oxford: Blackwell.

Harvey, D. 2005. *A brief history of neoliberalism*. Oxford; New York: Oxford University Press.

Hau, H. and M. Thum. 2009. Subprime crisis and board (in-)competence: private versus public banks in Germany. *Economic Policy* 24:701–752.

Haverland, M. 2001. Another Dutch miracle? Explaining Dutch and German pension trajectories. *Journal of European Social Policy* 11:308–323.

Hawley, J. and A. Williams. 2000. *The rise of fiduciary capitalism: how institutional investors can make corporate America more democratic*. Philadelphia, PA: University of Pennsylvania Press.

Hawley, J. and A. Williams. 2007. Universal owners: challenges and opportunities. *Corporate Governance: An International Review* 15:415–420.

Hay, C. 2004. Common trajectories, variable paces, divergent outcomes? Models of European capitalism under conditions of complex economic interdependence. *Review of International Political Economy* 11:262–262.

Heclo, H. 1974. *Modern social politics in Britain and Sweden: from relief to income maintenance*. New Haven, CT: Yale University Press.

Helleiner, E. 1994. *States and the reemergence of global finance: from Bretton Woods to the 1990s*. Ithaca, NY; London: Cornell University Press.

Henderson, J., P. Dicken, M. Hess, N. Coe, and H. Yeung. 2002. Global production networks and the analysis of economic development. *Review of International Political Economy* 9:436–464.

Hess, M. 2004. 'Spatial' relationships? Towards a reconceptualization of embeddedness. *Progress in Human Geography* 28:165–186.

Hess, M. and H. Yeung. 2006. Whither global production networks in economic geography? Past, present, and future. *Environment and Planning A* 38:1193–1204.

Hirst, P. and G. Thompson. 1999. *Globalization in question: the international economy and the possibilities of governance*. Cambridge: Polity Press.

Hobsbawm, E. 1987. *The age of empire, 1875–1914*. London: Weidenfeld and Nicolson.

Hollingsworth, J.R. and R. Boyer (eds). 1997. *Contemporary capitalism: the embeddedness of institutions*. Cambridge: Cambridge University Press.

Holzmann, R. and R.P. Hinz. 2005. *Old-age income support in the 21st century: an international perspective on pension systems and reform*. Washington, DC: World Bank.

Höpner, M. and G. Jackson. 2006. Revisiting the Mannesmann takeover: how markets for corporate control emerge. *European Management Review* 3:142–155.

Howard, C. 2007. *The welfare state nobody knows: debunking myths about U.S. social policy*. Princeton, NJ: Princeton University Press.

Howell, C. 2003. Varieties of capitalism: and then there was one? *Comparative Politics* 36:103–124.

Immergluck, D. 2004. *Credit to the community: community reinvestment and fair lending policy in the United States*. Armonk, NY; London: M.E. Sharpe.

Immergut, E., K. Anderson, and I. Schulze (eds). 2007. *The handbook of West European pension politics*. Oxford: Oxford University Press.

Jackson, G. and R. Deeg. 2008. From comparing capitalisms to the politics of institutional change. *Review of International Political Economy* 15:680–709.

Jacoby, S.M. 1997. *Modern manors: welfare capitalism since the New Deal*. Princeton, NJ: Princeton University Press.

Jensen, M.C. 1993. The modern industrial-revolution, exit, and the failure of internal control-systems. *Journal of Finance* 48:831–880.

Jensen, M.C. 2000. *A theory of the firm: governance, residual claims, and organizational forms*. Cambridge, MA: Harvard University Press.

Jessop, B., N. Brenner, and M. Jones. 2008. Theorizing sociospatial relations. *Environment and Planning D: Society and Space* 26:389–401.

Johal, S. and A. Leaver. 2007. Is the stock market a disciplinary institution? French giant firms and the regime of accumulation. *New Political Economy* 12:349–367.

Jones, A. 2008. Beyond embeddedness: economic practices and the invisible dimensions of transnational business activity. *Progress in Human Geography* 32:71–88.

Jones, G. 2005. *Multinationals and global capitalism: from the nineteenth to the twenty-first century*. Oxford: Oxford University Press.

Jones, K.D. and T. Critchfield. 2005. Consolidation in the U.S. banking industry: is the "long, strange trip" about to end? *FDIC Banking Review* 17:31–61.

Keynes, J.M. 1936. *The general theory of employment, interest and money.* London: Macmillan.

Kickert, W.J.M. 2003. Beneath consensual corporatism: traditions of governance in the Netherlands. *Public Administration* 81:119–140.

Kirchner, C. and R.W. Painter. 2002. Takeover defenses under Delaware law, the proposed Thirteenth EU Directive and the new German takeover law: comparison and recommendations for reform. *American Journal of Comparative Law* 50:451–476.

Kitschelt, H., P. Lange, G. Marks, and J. Stephens (eds). 1999. *Continuity and change in contemporary capitalism.* Cambridge: Cambridge University Press.

Klagge, B. and R. Martin. 2005. Decentralized versus centralized financial systems: is there a case for local capital markets? *Journal of Economic Geography* 5:387–421.

Klumpes, P., Y. Li, and M. Whittington. 2007. *The impact of UK pension accounting rule change on pension curtail decisions.* SSRN eLibrary.

Knorr-Cetina, K. and A. Preda (eds). 2005. *The sociology of financial markets.* Oxford: Oxford University Press.

Kobeissi, N. 2009. Impact of the Community Reinvestment Act on new business start-ups and economic growth in local markets. *Journal of Small Business Management* 47:489–513.

La Porta, R., F. Lopez-De-Silanes, and A. Shleifer. 1999. Corporate ownership around the world. *Journal of Finance* 54:471–517.

La Porta, R., F. Lopez-de-Silanes, A. Shleifer, and R. Vishny. 2000. Investor protection and corporate governance. *Journal of Financial Economics* 58:3–27.

La Porta, R., F. Lopez-De-Silanes, A. Shleifer, and R.W. Vishny. 1997. Legal determinants of external finance. *Journal of Finance* 52:1131–1150.

Lamfalussy, A. 2001. Towards an integrated European financial market. *World Economy* 24:1287–1294.

Lane, P.R. and G.M. Milesi-Ferretti. 2007. The external wealth of nations mark II: revised and extended estimates of foreign assets and liabilities, 1970–2004. *Journal of International Economics* 73:223–250.

Lane, P.R. and G.M. Milesi-Ferretti. 2008. The drivers of financial globalization. *American Economic Review* 98:327–332.

Langley, P. 2008. *The everyday life of global finance: saving and borrowing in Anglo-America.* Oxford: Oxford University Press.

Lazear, E.P. 1990. Pensions and deferred benefits as strategic compensation. *Industrial Relations* 29:263–280.

Lee, R., G.L. Clark, J. Pollard, and A. Leyshon. 2009. The remit of financial geography—before and after the crisis. *Journal of Economic Geography* 9:723–747.

Levine, R. 1997. Financial development and economic growth: views and agenda. *Journal of Economic Literature* 35:688–726.

Levy, J. 1999. *Tocqueville's revenge: state, society, and economy in contemporary France.* Cambridge, MA; London: Harvard University Press.

Levy, J. (ed.). 2006. *The state after statism: new state activities in the age of liberalization.* Cambridge, MA; London: Harvard University Press.

Leyshon, A. and N.J. Thrift. 1997. *Moneyspace: geographies of monetary transformation.* London: Routledge.

Leyshon, A. and N. Thrift. 2007. The capitalization of almost everything: the future of finance and capitalism. *Theory, Culture & Society* 24:97–115.

Leyshon, A., S. French, and P. Signoretta. 2008. Financial exclusion and the geography of bank and building society branch closure in Britain. *Transactions of the Institute of British Geographers* 33:447–465.

Lundvall, B. 1992. *National systems of innovation: towards a theory of innovation and interactive learning.* London: Pinter.

Lütz, S. 2004. Convergence within national diversity: the regulatory state in finance. *Journal of Public Policy* 24:169–197.

Maalouf, K. 2006. Impediments to financial development in the banking sector: a comparison of the impact of federalism in the United States and Germany. *Michigan Journal of International Law* 28:431–467.

McCann, P. 2008. Globalization and economic geography: the world is curved, not flat. *Cambridge Journal of Regions, Economy and Society* 1:351–370.

McKinnon, R. 1991. *The order of economic liberalization: financial control in the transition to a market economy.* Baltimore, MD: Johns Hopkins University Press.

Maddison, A. 1991. *Dynamic forces in capitalist development: a long-run comparative view.* Oxford: Oxford University Press.

Malmberg, A. and P. Maskell. 2006. Localized learning revisited. *Growth and Change* 37:1–18.

Marglin, S. and J. Schor (eds). 1990. *The golden age of capitalism: reinterpreting the postwar experience.* Oxford; New York: Oxford University Press.

Markowitz, H. 1952. Portfolio selection. *Journal of Finance* 7:77–91.

Markusen, A. 1985. *Profit cycles, oligopoly, and regional development.* Cambridge, MA; London: MIT Press.

Marshall, A. 1920. *Principles of economics: an introductory volume.* London: Macmillan.

Marshall, T.H. 1950. *Citizenship and social class, and other essays.* Cambridge: Cambridge University Press.

Marsico, R. 2004. Democratizing capital: the history, law and reform of the Community Reinvestment Act. *New York Law School Law Review* 49:717–726.

Martin, R. (ed.). 1999. *Money and the space economy*. Chichester: Wiley.

Martin, R. 2011. The local geographies of the financial crisis: from the housing bubble to economic recession and beyond. *Journal of Economic Geography* 11:587–618.

Martin, R. and P. Sunley. 2006. Path dependence and regional economic evolution. *Journal of Economic Geography* 6:395–437.

Martin, R., C. Berndt, B. Klagge, and P. Sunley. 2005. Spatial proximity effects and regional equity gaps in the venture capital market: evidence from Germany and the United Kingdom. *Environment and Planning A* 37:1207–1231.

Maskell, P. 2001. The firm in economic geography. *Economic Geography* 77:329–344.

Maskell, P. and A. Malmberg. 1999. Localised learning and industrial competitiveness. *Cambridge Journal of Economics* 23:167–185.

Massey, D. 1984. *Spatial divisions of labour: social structures and the geography of production*. London: Macmillan.

Memmel, C., C. Schmieder, and I. Stein. 2008. Relationship lending— empirical evidence for Germany. *European Investment Bank, Economic and Financial Report 2008/01*.

Merton, R.C. 1995a. A functional perspective of financial intermediation. *Financial Management* 24:23–41.

Merton, R.C. 1995b. Financial innovation and the management and regulation of financial institutions. *Journal of Banking & Finance* 19:461–481.

Merton, R.C. and Z. Bodie. 2005. Design of financial systems: towards a synthesis of structure and function. *Journal of Investment Management* 3:1–23.

Minns, R. 2001. *The cold war in welfare: stock markets versus pensions*. London: Verso.

Mitchell, K. 1995. Flexible circulation in the Pacific Rim: capitalism in cultural context. *Economic Geography* 71:364–382.

Monk, A.H.B. 2008. The knot of contracts: the corporate geography of legacy costs. *Economic Geography* 84:211–235.

Monk, A.H.B. 2009a. The financial thesis: reconceptualizing globalisation's effect on firms and institutions. *Competition & Change* 13:51–74.

Monk, A.H.B. 2009b. The geography of pension liabilities and fund governance in the United States. *Environment and Planning A* 41:859–878.

Morgan, G., R. Whitley, and E. Moen (eds). 2005. *Changing capitalisms?: internationalization, institutional change, and systems of economic organization.* Oxford: Oxford University Press.

Mouck, T. 2004. Institutional reality, financial reporting and the rules of the game. *Accounting, Organizations and Society* 29:525–541.

Mügge, D. 2006. Reordering the marketplace: competition politics in European finance. *Journal of Common Market Studies* 44:991–1022.

Munnell, A.H. and A.E. Sunden. 2004. *Coming up short: the challenge of 401(k) plans.* Washington, DC: Brookings Institution Press.

Myers, S.C. 1984. The capital structure puzzle. *Journal of Finance* 39:575–592.

Myles, J. and P. Pierson. 2001. The comparative political economy of pension reform. In *The new politics of the welfare state*, ed. P. Pierson, 305–333. Oxford: Oxford University Press.

North, D. 1990. *Institutions, institutional change, and economic performance.* Cambridge; New York: Cambridge University Press.

Nyce, S.A. and S.J. Schieber. 2005. *The economic implications of aging societies: the costs of living happily ever after.* Cambridge: Cambridge University Press.

Obinger, H., P. Starke, J. Moser, C. Bogedan, E. Gindulis, and S. Leibfried. 2010. *Transformations of the welfare state: small states, big lessons.* Oxford: Oxford University Press.

O'Brien, R. 1992. *Global financial integration: the end of geography.* London: Royal Institute of International Affairs; Pinter Publishers.

Ohmae, K. 1990. *The borderless world: power and strategy in the interlinked economy.* London: Collins.

Olds, K. 2001. *Globalization and urban change: capital, culture and Pacific Rim mega projects.* New York: Oxford University Press.

Omtzigt, P.H. 2007. Mandatory participation for companies. In *Costs and benefits of collective pension systems*, ed. O.W. Steenbeck and S. Van DerLecq, 187–201. Berlin: Springer-Verlag.

Orenstein, M.A. 2008. *Privatizing pensions: the transnational campaign for social security reform.* Princeton, NJ; Oxford: Princeton University Press.

O'Sullivan, M. 2000. *Contests for corporate control: corporate governance and economic performance in the United States and Germany.* Oxford: Oxford University Press.

Pagano, M., F. Panetta, and A.L. Zingales. 1998. Why do companies go public? An empirical analysis. *Journal of Finance* 53:27–64.

Palacios, R. 2003. Securing public pension promises through funding. In *The pension challenge: risk transfers and retirement income security*, ed. O.S. Mitchell and K.A. Smetters, 116–158. Oxford: Oxford University Press.

Palier, B. 2003. Facing the pension crisis in France. In Pension security in the 21st century: redrawing the public-private debate, ed. G.L. Clark and N. Whiteside, 93–114. Oxford: Oxford University Press.

Palier, B. and G. Bonoli. 2000. La montée en puissance des fonds de pension: une lecture comparative des réformes des systèmes de retraite, entre modèle global et cheminements nationaux. *L'Année de la Régulation* 4:209–250.

Patrick, H. 1966. Financial development and economic growth in underdeveloped countries. *Economic Development and Cultural Change* 14:174–189.

Peck, J. 1996. *Work-place: the social regulation of labor markets*. New York; London: Guilford Press.

Peck, J. 2010. *Constructions of neoliberal reason*. Oxford: Oxford University Press.

Peck, J. and N. Theodore. 2007. Variegated capitalism. *Progress in Human Geography* 31:731–772.

Peck, J. and J. Zhang. 2013. A variety of capitalism...with Chinese characteristics? *Journal of Economic Geography* 13:357–396.

Pemberton, H. 2006. Politics and pensions in post-war Britain. In *Britain's pension crisis: history and policy*, ed. H. Pemberton, P. Thane, and N. Whiteside, 39–63. Oxford: Oxford University Press.

Phelps, N.A. 2008. Cluster or capture? Manufacturing foreign direct investment, external economies and agglomeration. *Regional Studies* 42:457–473.

Pierson, P. 2004. *Politics in time: history, institutions, and social analysis*. Princeton, NJ; Oxford: Princeton University Press.

Plender, J. 1986. London's Big Bang in international context. *International Affairs* 63:39–48.

Pollard, J.S. 2003. Small firm finance and economic geography. *Journal of Economic Geography* 3:429–452.

Ponds, E. and B. van Riel. 2009. Sharing risk: the Netherlands' new approach to pensions. *Journal of Pension Economics and Finance* 8:91–105.

Pontusson, J. 2005. *Inequality and prosperity: social Europe vs. liberal America*. Ithaca, NY; London: Cornell University Press.

Prantl, S., M. Almus, J. Egeln, and D. Engel. 2009. Kreditvergabe durch Genossenschaftsbanken, Kreditbanken und Sparkassen: Eine empirische Analyse von Föderkrediten für junge, kleine Unternehmen. *Schmollers Jahrbuch* 129:83–132.

Queisser, M., E. Whitehouse, and P. Whiteford. 2007. The public–private pension mix in OECD countries. *Industrial Relations Journal* 38:542–568.

Rajan, R.G. 1992. Insiders and outsiders: the choice between informed and arm's-length debt. *Journal of Finance* 47:1367–1400.

Rajan, R.G. and L. Zingales. 1995. What do we know about capital structure? Some evidence from international data. *Journal of Finance* 50:1421–1460.

Rajan, R.G. and L. Zingales. 2003. Banks and markets: the changing character of European finance. In *The transformation of the European financial system*, ed. V. Gaspar, P. Hartmann, and O. Sleijpan, 123–167. Frankfurt am Main: European Central Bank (ECB).

Rauh, J.D. 2006. Investment and financing constraints: evidence from the funding of corporate pension plans. *Journal of Finance* 61:33–71.

Robinson, J. 1952. *The rate of interest, and other essays*. London: Macmillan.

Rodríguez-Pose, A. and R. Crescenzi. 2008. Mountains in a flat world: why proximity still matters for the location of economic activity. *Cambridge Journal of Regions, Economy and Society* 1:371–388.

Rodríguez-Pose, A. and M. Storper. 2006. Better rules or stronger communities? On the social foundations of institutional change and its economic effects. *Economic Geography* 82:1–25.

Roe, M. 2012. Corporate short-termism in the fiscal cliff's shadow. *Project Syndicate* Dec 20, 3.

Roe, M.J. 2003. *Political determinants of corporate governance: political context, corporate impact*. Oxford; New York: Oxford University Press.

Sarre, P. 2007. Understanding the geography of international finance. *Geography Compass* 1:1076–1096.

Sass, S.A. 1997. *The promise of private pensions: the first hundred years*. Cambridge, MA: Harvard University Press.

Sassen, S. 2001. *The global city: New York, London, Tokyo*. Princeton, NJ: Princeton University Press.

Saxenian, A. 1994. *Regional advantage: culture and competition in Silicon Valley and Route 128*. Cambridge, MA; London: Harvard University Press.

Saxenian, A. 2006. *The new argonauts: regional advantage in a global economy*. Cambridge, MA; London: Harvard University Press.

Scammell, W.M. 1980. *The international economy since 1945*. London: Macmillan.

Schmidt, V. 2002. *The futures of European capitalism*. Oxford: Oxford University Press.

Schmidt, V. 2003. French capitalism transformed, but still a third variety of capitalism. *Economy and Society* 32:526–554.

Schoenberger, E. 1997. *The cultural crisis of the firm*. Cambridge, MA; Oxford: Blackwell Publishers.

Schoenberger, E. 2000. The management of time and space. In *The Oxford handbook of economic geography*, ed. G.L. Clark, M. Gertler, and M. Feldman, 317–332. Oxford: Oxford University Press.

Schumpeter, J. 1934. *The theory of economic development: an inquiry into profits, capital, credit, interest, and the business cycle*. Cambridge, MA: Harvard University Press.

Scott, A.J. 1998. *Regions and the world economy: the coming shape of global production, competition, and political order*. Oxford: Oxford University Press.

Scott, A.J. 2000. Economic geography: the great half-century. In *The Oxford handbook of economic geography*, ed. G.L. Clark, M. Gertler, and M. Feldman, 18–44. Oxford: Oxford University Press.

Scott, A.J. 2006. *Geography and economy: three lectures*. Oxford: Clarendon Press.

Scott, A.J. 2012. *A world in emergence: cities and regions in the 21st century*. Cheltenham: Edward Elgar.

Scott, A.J. and M. Storper. 1987. High technology industry and regional development: a theoretical critique and reconstruction. *International Social Science Journal* 39:215–232.

Scott, A.J. and M. Storper. 2003. Regions, globalization, development. *Regional Studies* 37:549–578.

Scott, W.R. 2008. *Institutions and organizations*. Thousand Oaks, CA; London: Sage.

Searle, J.R. 1995. *The construction of social reality*. London: Allen Lane.

Sheppard, E. 2011. Geographical political economy. *Journal of Economic Geography* 11:319–331.

Sheppard, E. 2012. Trade, globalization and uneven development: entanglements of geographical political economy. *Progress in Human Geography* 36:44–71.

Shonfield, A. 1965. *Modern capitalism: the changing balance of public and private power*. London: Oxford University Press.

Sinn, H.-W. 1999. *The German state banks: global players in the international financial markets*. Cheltenham: Edward Elgar.

Sorge, A. 2005. *The global and the local: understanding the dialectics of business systems*. Oxford; New York: Oxford University Press.

Stiglitz, J. 1989. Financial markets and development. *Oxford Review of Economic Policy* 5:55–68.

Storper, M. 1997. *The regional world: territorial development in a global economy*. New York; London: Guilford Press.

Storper, M. 2011. Why do regions develop and change? The challenge for geography and economics. *Journal of Economic Geography* 11:333–346.

Storper, M. and R. Walker. 1989. *The capitalist imperative: territory, technology, and industrial growth*. Oxford: Basil Blackwell.

Story, J. and I. Walter. 1997. *Political economy of financial integration in Europe: the battle of the systems*. Manchester: Manchester Universtiy Press.

Stout, L. 2012. *The shareholder value myth: how putting shareholders first harms investors, corporations, and the public*. San Francisco, CA: Berrett-Koehler.

Strange, S. 1976. *International economic relations of the western world, 1959–1971*. London; New York: Published for the Royal Institute of International Affairs by Oxford University Press.

Streeck, W. 2009. *Re-forming capitalism: institutional change in the German political economy*. Oxford: Oxford University Press.

Streeck, W. 2011. Institutions in history: bringing capitalism back in. In *The Oxford handbook of comparative institutional analysis*, ed. G. Morgan, J.L. Campbell, C. Crouch, O.K. Pedersen, and R. Whitely, 659–686. Oxford: Oxford University Press.

Streeck, W. and K. Thelen (eds). 2005. *Beyond continuity: institutional change in advanced political economies*. Oxford: Oxford University Press.

Streeck, W. and K. Yamamura (eds). 2001. *The origins of nonliberal capitalism: Germany and Japan in comparison*. Ithaca, NY; London: Cornell University Press.

Sunley, P. 2008. Relational economic geography: a partial understanding or a new paradigm? *Economic Geography* 84:1–26.

Sunley, P., B. Klagge, C. Berndt, and R. Martin. 2005. Venture capital programmes in the UK and Germany: in what sense regional policies? *Regional Studies* 39:255–273.

Swank, D. 2002. *Global capital, political institutions, and policy change in developed welfare states*. Cambridge: Cambridge University Press.

Swinkels, L. 2011. Have pension plans changed after the introduction of IFRS? *Pensions* 16:244–255.

Taylor, J. and J. Silver. 2008. The Community Reinvestment Act at 30: looking back looking to the future. *New York Law School Law Review* 53:203–225.

Taylor, M. and P. Oinas (eds). 2006. *Understanding the firm: spatial and organizational dimensions*. Oxford: Oxford University Press.

Taylor, P.J. 1994. The state as container: territoriality in the modern world-system. *Progress in Human Geography* 18:151–162.

Taylor, P.J. 1995. Beyond containers: internationality, interstateness, interterritoriality. *Progress in Human Geography* 19:1–15.

Taylor-Gooby, P. (ed.). 2004. *New risks, new welfare: the transformation of the European welfare state*. Oxford: Oxford University Press.

Thelen, K. 2004. *How institutions evolve: the political economy of skills in Germany, Britain, the United States, and Japan*. Cambridge: Cambridge University Press.

Thrift, N.J. 2005. *Knowing capitalism*. London: Sage.

Toporowski, J. 2000. *The end of finance: the theory of capital market inflation, financial derivatives and pension fund capitalism*. London: Routledge.

Udell, G.F. 2008. What's in a relationship? The case of commercial lending. *Business Horizons* 51:93–103.

Van Ewijk, C. 2005. Reform of occupational pensions in the Netherlands. *De Economist* 153:331–347.

Vernon, R. 1971. *Sovereignty at bay: the multinational spread of U.S. enterprises*. New York; London: Basic Books.

Vitols, S. 2005. Changes in Germany's bank-based financial system: implications for corporate governance. *Corporate Governance: An International Review* 13:386–396.

Waine, B. 1995. A disaster foretold? The case of the personal pension. *Social Policy & Administration* 29:317–334.

Wallerstein, I. 2004. *World-systems analysis: an introduction*. Durham, NC; London: Duke University Press.

Webber, M. and D. Rigby. 1996. *The golden age illusion: rethinking postwar capitalism*. New York: Guilford Press.

Whiteford, P. and E. Whitehouse. 2006. Pension challenges and pension reforms in OECD countries. *Oxford Review of Economic Policy* 22:78–94.

Whiteside, N. 2006. Adapting private pensions to public purposes: historical perspectives on the politics of reform. *Journal of European Social Policy* 16:43–54.

Whitley, R. 1999. *Divergent capitalisms: the social structuring and change of business systems*. Oxford: Oxford University Press.

Whitley, R. 2007. *Business systems and organizational capabilities: the institutional structuring of competitive competences*. Oxford: Oxford University Press.

Whittington, G. 2008. Fair value and the IASB/FASB conceptual framework project: an alternative view. *Abacus* 44:139–168.

Whittington, R. and M. Mayer. 2000. *The European corporation: strategy, structure, and social science*. Oxford: Oxford University Press.

Williamson, O. 1985. *The economic institutions of capitalism: firms, markets, relational contracting.* New York: Free Press.

Wójcik, D. 2002. Cross-border corporate ownership and capital market integration in Europe: evidence from portfolio and industrial holdings. *Journal of Economic Geography* 2:455–491.

Wójcik, D. 2006. Convergence in corporate governance: evidence from Europe and the challenge for economic geography. *Journal of Economic Geography* 6:639–660.

Wójcik, D. 2011. *The global stock market: issuers, investors, and intermediaries in an uneven world.* Oxford: Oxford University Press.

World Bank. 1994. *Averting the old age crisis: policies to protect the old and promote growth.* Oxford: Oxford University Press.

Yamamura, K. and W. Streeck (eds). 2003. *The end of diversity? Prospects for German and Japanese capitalism.* Ithaca, NY; London: Cornell University Press.

Yeung, H. 2005. The firm as social networks: an organisational perspective. *Growth and Change* 36:307–328.

Zook, M.A. 2002. Grounded capital: venture financing and the geography of the Internet industry, 1994–2000. *Journal of Economic Geography* 2:151–177.

Zysman, J. 1983. *Governments, markets and growth: financial systems and the politics of industrial change.* Oxford: Robertson.

Index

Printed and bound by CPI Group (UK) Ltd, Croydon, CR0 4YY